STONESCAPING
IDEA BOOK

STONESCAPING
IDEA BOOK

ANDREW WORMER

The Taunton Press

To Dwight (who recognized my true potential, yet hired me anyway)

The Taunton Press
Inspiration for hands-on living®

The Taunton Press, Inc., 63 South Main Street, PO Box 5506, Newtown, CT 06470-5506
e-mail: tp@taunton.com

Editor: Mindy Fox
Interior Design and Layout: David Giammattei
Illustrator: Christine Erikson
Cover Photographers: FRONT COVER (top row, left to right): © Brian Vanden Brink;
© Lisa Romerein; © Brian Vanden Brink; Virginia Small, © The Taunton Press, Inc.;
(middle row, left to right): © Lee Anne White; © Lee Anne White; © Steve Vierra;
Allan Mandell, © The Taunton Press, Inc.; (bottom row, left to right): © Brian Vanden Brink;
© Steve Vierra; © Mark Samu; © Lee Anne White; BACK COVER (top left) Jennifer Benner,
© The Taunton Press, Inc.; (bottom row, left to right) all photos © Lee Anne White.

Library of Congress Cataloging-in-Publication Data
Wormer, Andrew.
 Stonescaping idea book / Andrew Wormer.
    p. cm.
 ISBN-13: 978-1-56158-763-6
 ISBN-10: 1-56158-763-X
 1. Stone in landscape gardening. I. Title.
 SB475.5W67 2005
 717--dc22
                              2005011614

Printed in China
10 9 8 7 6

Acknowledgments

I think one of the attractions of stone is that it offers almost immediate gratification: Like many others, I just find it very satisfying to pick up an interesting rock, handle and inspect it, maybe even put it in my pocket and carry it around with me for a while. But creating artful and enduring landscape designs with stone is another matter; bigger stones are heavy and unwieldy to work with, demanding—and rewarding—patience, a skilled eye, and (if you're the one actually installing it) a strong back. In the course of writing this book, I've been fortunate to be able to speak with a number of knowledgeable individuals who have some combination—or all—of these attributes.

Whether the conversation was an informal one that took place at a stone yard or landscaping supply store or a lengthy interview in person or over the phone, these experts generously shared their enthusiasm and appreciation for this most ancient of building materials. In addition to their insights, many of them contributed examples of their work

to this book, and they're listed in the credits at the back. But others contributed ideas and guidance that are harder to credit; in some cases, I've also received photos from these individuals that, while they couldn't be published, gave me a broader understanding of the various ways that stone is being used in contemporary landscape design. I'd particularly like to thank Tim and Lisa Goodman of Goodman Landscape Design in Berkeley, California; David Raphael of Land-Works in Middlebury, Vermont; Elizabeth Webb of Hepatica in Bristol, Vermont; Bob George of That's Landscaping in Croton-on-Hudson, New York; Lou French in Vineyard Haven, Massachusetts; Jeffrey Bale in Portland, Oregon; Catherine Clemens of Clemens and Associates in Santa Fe, New Mexico; David Hawk of Hawk Design in Charlestown, Massachusetts; Kris Horiuchi of Horiuchi & Solien in Falmouth, Massachusetts; and Sharon Coates of Zaretsky and Associates in Rochester, New York.

Once again, I've relied on some great photographers to bring the work of the designers and builders to my attention and to life. Special thanks go to Carolyn Bates, Lee Anne White, and Brian Vanden Brink, who not only contributed the bulk of the images used in the book, but who also were particularly helpful in providing background information and who put me in touch with some terrific landscape designers and stone masons.

And though Taunton keeps on mixing me up by adding new people to their talented team, they still manage to get the job done. Thanks again to Carolyn Mandarano, Julie Hamilton, and Jenny Peters, who nursed this project along, and especially to Mindy Fox, who rearranged my words so that they made sense to others besides myself.

Contents

Introduction

Back in the 1970s, it was fashionable to spend some time "finding oneself" after graduating from college. So, not long after pocketing my newly minted bachelor's degree in English, I joined a landscaping crew instead of pursuing a more traditional career. While most of our duties seemed to revolve around pushing lawnmowers, we occasionally worked on more interesting projects, including a few that involved the use of stone. At the time, the material seemed to require a lot more labor than my 21-year-old mind thought it was worth, particularly on those very hot days when a truckload or more would show up on our job site, or when the client seemed overly particular about just how the stone should be placed.

Over the years, I've developed a keener appreciation for stone and the various roles that it can play in the landscape. Though carpentry has become my trade, and journalism my profession, stone has come to play a central role in my life. In Vermont, where I live, old stone walls abound, and quarries continue to produce slate, granite, and marble, just as they have for over two hundred years. The lakes my family swim in are notable for their rocky outcroppings and shale and cobble shorelines; a sandy beach is a rarity here. We fish in beautiful, boulder-strewn streams, and hike on paths and ski on slopes that often seem to be carved from stone.

Even our house pays homage to stone: its foundation is built directly onto bedrock. Walk down into our basement and you'll step onto the smooth ledge outcropping that passes directly beneath our home. Besides underpinning our dwelling, granite ledges surround it. With them, we've created informal, low stone walls and borders for our gardens. From time to time, I walk out into the woods that surround our home with my pry bar and unearth new candidates, ensuring that our borders continue to slowly grow.

We are, quite literally, surrounded by stone. But we're ready to go a step further, too. We have some informal flagstone paths that need attention, a gravel driveway that we'd like to redo, and a spot on our property that

needs a proper retaining wall. And we'd like to add on a new outdoor room, a place where we can gather and comfortably enjoy those balmy Vermont summer evenings.

Maybe you're like me, looking for practical solutions to particular landscaping problems. Or maybe you've seen a stunning wall or walkway somewhere that you think would look great at your home. Maybe you're putting in a swimming pool and would like to make it look like a more natural part of your landscape. Or maybe your budget is more limited, but you still love the look and sound of water moving over rocks. The right kind of stone will help you achieve your goals; all you need are some ideas to help you figure out how

you'll use it. That's where this book comes in.

Here you'll be presented with a range of practical and inspiring ideas for using stone in your landscape. Along with tried-and-true designs for inviting walkways and beautiful walls, you'll see new ways of using stone in gardens and patio spaces. You'll discover ideas for creating graceful streams, waterfalls, and even simple fountains that will help transform your backyard into a private retreat. And you'll find a wide range of outdoor living spaces that family and friends can enjoy for years to come. As the examples in the book will demonstrate, there is a world of stone to explore; use this book to help get you started on the right path.

Paths and Steps

W alks, pathways, and steps play important roles around the exterior of the home. On a practical level, they offer a safe and comfortable means of approaching your house in all seasons and weather conditions. They also serve to connect your house with its surrounding landscape, providing a logical route to frequently used areas such as garages and outbuildings, or a more meandering route through gardens.

But as we all know, the journey can be at least as important as the destination. As pathways weave through trees and around obstacles, stepping up or down as the grade changes, they become part of the landscape. A properly planned pathway is a place of discovery: Our feet move us along the path while hidden places or scenic vistas are revealed to our eyes.

Durable and versatile, stone is perfectly suited for building beautiful paths and steps. Cut stone has a formal elegance, making it a good choice for main pathways and stairs, while the random shapes and aged surfaces of natural stone give it a more relaxed informality.

◄ AN ENTRYWAY PAVED with native island stone taken from the fields surrounding this vintage 1730s Martha's Vineyard farm matches the homestead's rugged and rustic ambience. Groundcovers, moss, and lichen soften the stone and contribute to the landscape's weathered look.

Paths

WHEN DECIDING ON A PARTICULAR TYPE OF STONE for a path, consider first your pathway's location in the landscape and its purpose. Functional paths—that is, pathways leading to the house or from the house to the garage, for example—tend to follow a direct route and should be wide enough for two people to walk side by side and smooth enough so that walkers don't have to focus on their footwork. Here is where the even surfaces and regular shapes of cut stones can be used to best advantage. On narrower, less formal secondary paths—such as those that lead to rear entries or through a garden—traffic tends to move more slowly. The irregular surfaces, random shapes, and varied colors of flagstone and fieldstone can be used to encourage a more leisurely pace.

▲ A WINDING PATH composed of large slabs of field-stone leads through the guesthouse garden of this ocean-front home on Martha's Vineyard. The irregular shaped stone was used to create curving paths through informal garden spaces, encouraging a contemplative pace.

► COMPOSED OF SQUARE-CUT SLABS that offer a perfect balance of formal and informal, this stepping-stone path leads gently through a garden of lush hydrangea, allowing its homeowner to venture out for cuttings in any weather without muddying her feet.

▲ AN EYE-CATCHING MOSAIC CREATED from stones and pebbles chosen for their size, shape, and color provides this garden path with an intriguing focal point.

School of Rock

WHEN CHOOSING STONE, **several factors will influence your decision, including color, style, texture, durability, and price. Here's a brief description of the three basic types of rock:**

- **Sedimentary rocks are formed in layers, so they split naturally into flat pieces, making them the most popular type of stone for landscaping. Examples include sandstone, limestone, and shale.**
- **Igneous rocks, like granite and basalt, are formed by volcanic activity and are dense and heavy.**
- **Metamorphic rocks, such as marble, are also hard and heavy. They're formed when sedimentary rocks are transformed by a combination of heat, pressure, and, sometimes, chemical interaction.**

▼ LOCALLY KNOWN AS BOTH Rocky Mountain quartzite and mica slate (but actually neither slate nor quartzite), the pathway flagstone used for the Japanese-influenced main entry to this Oregon home has an Asian character. The stone was chosen for its color, smooth surface, and relatively modest cost.

CUT-STONE PATHS

▶ A BORDER COMPOSED OF STONES set on edge helps hold this pathway together, clearly defines the edges of the planting beds, and mutes the somewhat commercial appearance of the concrete pavers while matching the stone slab steps leading up to the raised patio.

Stone Installation Options

WHILE CUT STONES CAN BE SET DIRECTLY in stable soil, usually it's better to either dry-lay them in sand or wet-lay them in mortar that's supported by concrete. In either case, your path needs to be supported by a foundation that provides a stable bed, aids in drainage, and—in cold climates—buffers the effects of freeze/thaw cycles.

There are advantages and disadvantages to each type of installation. The wet-mortar method (the most stable and permanent type) offers the best protection against frost heaves and weeds—provided, of course, that the base is

prepared properly. Because it requires a concrete foundation, this method is the most costly and labor-intensive.

A dry-laid a stone path can be nearly as stable as a path mortared on concrete, particularly if the stones you are working with are large or thick. An edging detail that helps holds the paving firmly in place will provide strength to the path's borders and help stabilize it, as will fairly tight, well-packed joints between the stones. An advantage to a dry-laid path is that individual stones are easily repaired or replaced if displaced or damaged by tree roots, frost, or drainage problems.

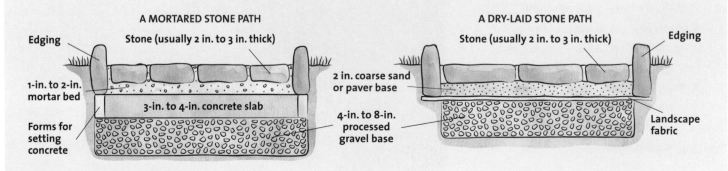

A MORTARED STONE PATH

Edging
Stone (usually 2 in. to 3 in. thick)
1-in. to 2-in. mortar bed
3-in. to 4-in. concrete slab
Forms for setting concrete

A DRY-LAID STONE PATH

Stone (usually 2 in. to 3 in. thick)
Edging
2 in. coarse sand or paver base
4-in. to 8-in. processed gravel base
Landscape fabric

About Bluestone

ONE OF THE MOST POPULAR landscaping stones, and a sound choice for walks and patios, is bluestone, a type of sandstone. Like all sandstones, bluestone is a soft, sedimentary rock with a natural grain that makes it relatively easy to shape, carve, and split into flat pieces.

Like all sandstones, bluestone varies widely in quality and strength depending on its geographical and geological location, so its long-term durability will largely depend on the particular quarry where it is found. Another determining factor is the climate where the stone will be installed. Areas with significant freeze/thaw cycles are tough on stone, and bluestone in particular tends to flake and chip away on the surface (called spalling). In milder climates, this is less of an issue.

By the way, bluestone isn't just blue. Colors range from lavender to rust to blue/gray, with significant variation in between (the color comes from the sand out of which the stone was formed). You can choose a particular color of bluestone, but expect to find some natural variation in hue within each flat or pallet that you purchase. Bluestone costs about $3 per square foot and up; you'll pay a premium for uniformly colored stone.

▲ A SEDIMENTARY STONE available in a range of colors including rust (center) and blue (left), bluestone is popular for walks and patios because of its natural flat surface, smooth texture, and reasonable cost.

▲ BECAUSE IT IS a relatively soft stone, bluestone can be readily cut into square or rectangular shapes. This bluestone paver has tumbled edges, giving it an antique quality.

▼ PART OF A STYLIZED stone garden "carpet," the S-curve cut into these large bluestone pavers is composed of terra cotta roof tiles taken from an old house that originally stood on the site.

About Stone Pavers

Rocks that have been split along the grain into a uniform (typically 1 ½ in.) thickness and that have been cut into a rectangular or square shape are called pavers. Pavers can be cut in a wide range of sizes from a variety of stone, including limestone, sandstone, granite, and slate. At a stone yard, you'll find that pavers are generally classified as either "random rectangular" or "cut-to-size." Starting at 12-in. square, random rectangular pavers range up to 24 in. by 36 in., in 6-in. increments in either length or width. All other sizes that have 90-degree corners are considered to be cut-to-size.

▲ A WALKWAY WITHOUT BORDERS to the side entryway to this Vermont home curves gently through bark-mulched planting beds. The path's Pennsylvania bluestone pavers have a smooth and durable surface that makes them easy to walk on and holds up well to New England's harsh climate.

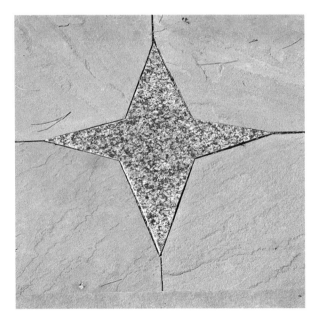

▲ A GIFT FROM THE STONEMASON to the home-owner, this insert marks a transition at the landing of a short flight of stairs leading to a sunken blue-stone patio. The insert is cut from Violetta granite, a stone often used for countertops.

▲ COMPOSED OF CUT SLATE in various sizes and hues, this short stone path's rich color and texture almost match the colorful plantings on either side. The path is wide, offering plenty of room for a couple to walk side by side.

▲ REFLECTING THE SHINGLE COTTAGE'S straightforward and unadorned exterior, this front entry path is composed of random rectangular cut-stone pavers.

NATURAL-STONE PATHS

▶ **STEPS ARE DELIBERATELY SLOWED** by the slightly irregular surface of this flagstone path, which leads down toward one of Martha's Vineyard's many salt ponds. Like the dry-stacked wall that flanks it, the path is built with stone imported from off-island, as native stone is scarce.

About Flagstone and Fieldstone

FLAT, IRREGULARLY SHAPED STONES are usually called flagstones, but this isn't a geological term. Flagstones, or "flags," are simply rocks that have been fractured, or cleft, into a reasonably flat profile, usually 1 in. to 2 in. thick, and that have uncut, natural edges. Like cut stones, flagstones are available in a wide range of rock varieties, including bluestone, slate, limestone, and granite. While some flagstones—such as slate and bluestone—split cleanly and have a smooth surface, other flagstones—such as limestone and quartzite—don't split quite so readily. Their surface can be roughly textured, which makes laying them into a relatively smooth path or patio challenging but also lends a rustic character to the final design.

Flagstones can also be cleft from fieldstone, a generic term that simply describes stone that is made up of a variety of minerals. These are the kinds of rocks that are naturally found in a given area—"out in the field" so to speak—and so the geological characteristics of fieldstone vary from region to region. This is what gives fieldstone its character, and some regions are known for their distinctive native varieties.

▶ **AVAILABLE IN A WIDE VARIETY OF STONES,** including slate (left), limestone (center), and quartzite (right), flagstones are characterized by their irregular shape and rough texture underfoot.

▲ A LUSH GREEN CARPET of blue star creeper (in bloom) and brass buttons spills out between the small flag-stones of this garden path. Both of these hardy ground covers stand up well to foot traffic and help to prevent erosion while blocking weed growth.

▲ LIKE A STREAMBED, rain brings out the color and texture of this garden path's pebbled surface.

▲ TO CREATE A COMPOSED rather than a contrived landscape, choose pathway stones that parallel the character of their surroundings. Smooth-cut stones would look out of place here, while the irregular stones used for this woodland pathway have a rugged look that matches the natural setting.

▶ BECAUSE THERE IS A GUEST-HOUSE that doubles as a home office at the end of this path, traffic is relatively heavy. These large, smooth Arizona Rose sandstone flags are easy to navigate; they also help hold moisture and nurture root growth for adjacent groundcover, a beneficial feature in Arizona's arid climate.

▲ WHEN HEAVY RAINS exposed hundreds of "potato stones" in a load of recently spread but not yet seeded topsoil, the homeowner picked them out one by one and started this stone path. Over the years, it's been expanded with smooth stone culled from local streambeds.

STEPPING-STONE PATHS

▼ STEPPING-STONE PATHS often function as borders between lawns and gardens. Instead of turf, try plantings between the stones, which help blur the boundaries, soften borders, and ease the transition between the two areas.

▲ A MEANDERING PATH wanders through paperbark birches, creating a woodland retreat in the backyard of this suburban Portland, Oregon, home. Closely spaced stepping stones help slow the pace as the walkway reaches its destination, a Colorado blue spruce.

Installing Stepping Stones in Turf

STEPPING STONES CAN EASILY BE INSTALLED after your site has been graded for a new lawn, but if your turf is already well-established, you can simply dig individual holes for each stone. First, position the stones for your path in a pleasing arrangement. Next, cut an outline around each stone with a sharp shovel and remove the sod where the stone will be located. Measure the thickness of your stone and excavate the hole to this depth plus an inch or so, which will leave enough room to add a thin layer of sand to "bed" the stone in. As you set the stone, twist it so that it settles into the sand, leveling it as necessary by adding or removing sand or using small rocks as shims.

Plantings for Stepping-Stone Paths

DIFFERENT TYPES OF PLANTS CAN BE SUCCESSFULLY ADDED to garden paths to soften the look of stone and give a natural look while easing the transition between gardens and lawns. At the same time, these plantings help to suppress weeds and prevent erosion.

Stepping-stone paths in particular are well suited for plantings. Just leave 3 in. or 4 in. of space between each stone filled with a 50/50 mixture of sand and topsoil to provide a good planting pocket for low-growing or creeping plants. Choose hardy perennials that stand up well to foot traffic, such as blue star creeper for heavily traveled paths, reserving less-hardy perennials, such as baby's tears, for pathways that see only occasional use (right). Experiment with a variety of midsize perennials, such as sedum, planting them along the edges of pathways to add variety and interest. Try adding fragrant herbs such as mint or thyme to your paths; they're hardy enough to thrive underfoot and will scent the air every time someone walks by (below). Before choosing plantings, you'll want to consider surrounding soil conditions and the amount of light, water, and use that your pathways receive.

▲ AS AN ALTERNATIVE TO GRASS, ground covers such as blue star creeper and baby's tears can be used to provide a lovely green border around a stepping-stone path.

▼ TO ADD COLOR, variety, and texture to your pathway, plant a mixture of low creepers like thyme or mint between the stones, allowing larger perennials such as sedum to spill in from the sides.

▶ ▼ THOUGH THE BULK OF SEASONAL DRAINAGE is handled by a larger dry creek bed on the other side of this Atlanta home, this pathway also sees some occasional overflow. Slate stepping stones set in pea gravel keep feet dry in wet weather while helping to hold the gravel from washing into the street (top right). The path passes through the arched gate and by the house, then ducks through a small pergola that was erected to provide privacy to a downstairs bathroom from a neighboring house (right). Cast concrete sand dollars from the homeowners previous residence personalize the path.

▶ TWISTING THROUGH A NARROW, rock-lined ravine overgrown with ferns and other foliage, this garden path creates a sense of mystery and suspense, only offering hints of the destination beyond.

◄ BECAUSE IT MEANDERS THROUGH this small garden rather than leads to a visible destination, this path invites the feet and eyes to linger and helps make this space feel larger.

▼ THOUGH DECIDEDLY INFORMAL, these stepping stones provide a clear sense of direction to the backyard of this Florida home.

GRAVEL AND MIXED-MATERIAL PATHS

▲ PERMANENTLY SET INTO MORTAR, this mosaic path is composed of a variety of different sizes, shapes, and colors of small pebbles carefully sorted into a streamlike arrangement. When creating a similar path or landing, wetting the stones before setting them brings out their colors, making it easier to arrange them into pleasing patterns.

▲ RECYCLED BRICK ARRANGED in a diagonal pattern outlines a path of stone and broken concrete, adding an element of surprise that also helps to make the narrow garden running along the side of the house feel wider.

▲ A DELICATE "STREAM" of Indonesian beach pebbles set in mortar meanders through an entryway paved with Arizona rose sandstone flagstones. The stone stream begins as a pool near the front door, drops down over a small flight of stairs, and eventually runs into an actual water fountain.

About Landscape Aggregates

LANDSCAPE AGGREGATES—LOOSE STONE or other inorganic materials less than 1 in. or so in diameter—can be used to create paths with a wide range of color and texture. Aggregates can be formal or informal, are economical and easy to install, and are forgiving of both tree roots and freeze/thaw cycles. Rough stones, such as crushed granite or lava rock, will compact into a relatively stable surface, while smoother stones, such as river rock, are harder to keep in place. Stones from 1/4 in. to 3/4 in. are best for walking comfort, and a good border design will help them stay put.

▲ A ROUND PEBBLE MOSAIC at the landing of a set of cast concrete stairs marks the transition to a pair of Tennessee fieldstone paths. Slender pieces of slate divide the mosaic into six pie-shaped sections, while the surrounding pea gravel helps drain water off of the path.

▲ A NETWORK OF PEA GRAVEL paths connects various types of garden spaces with one another around this Georgia home. This path assumes a more formal character as it's bordered by an alternating pattern of square and rectangular cut stone pavers. The brickwork capping the stone wall flanking the path reflects the all-brick facade of the main house, helping to unify the architecture with the landscape.

Steps

WHETHER YOUR LANDSCAPE ACTUALLY REQUIRES them or not, steps are a good idea. On a practical level, they can be used to provide a safe and comfortable means of changing from one level to another without slipping or sliding when the weather is wet and the conditions muddy. But steps and staircases can also be used to add an exciting design element to virtually any type of site, whether it is flat or hilly. The regular, horizontal lines of a set of stairs become a natural focal point that highlights topographical changes in the landscape, and when that focal point is composed in beautiful, timeless stone, the effect is magnified. Ranging from informal stepping stones cut into the face of a gently sloping hill to formal staircases with painstakingly laid risers and treads, stone stairs can be used in a variety of ways to dress up your landscape.

◀▼ AGED FIELDSTONE SLABS create a series of rustic entry steps that bisect a stone retaining wall and ascend through an informal garden built on a slope. The intermediate landings offer a place to pause and enjoy the gardens.

◄ FORMED CONCRETE stairs and cinder block retaining walls provide the structure for the landscape of this hillside California home, while veneered Connecticut bluestone steps and volcanic California fieldstones (aka moss rocks) lend a natural look. A fountain at the top of the stairs circulates water over the adjacent rock wall and back again.

▲ PORPHYRY IS A HARD volcanic rock with a distinctive color (it gets its name from the Greek word *porphyros*, for the color purple). Here it's been cut into regular bricklike pavers and larger treads for the stairs, creating a formal entry to this Santa Fe home.

◄ BUILT WITH RUBBLE ROCK excavated during construction, this cobbled stone stairway leads to a stone terrace adjacent to the kitchen of an Italian-style California villa. Chipped to fit and laid into cement to hold them securely, the stones were turned flat-side up to provide a smooth walking surface.

FORMAL STAIRWAYS

▶ USE CURVES AND CIRCULAR SHAPES as an alternative to rectilinear forms to add an element of mystery and surprise to a landscape. These stairs are cut from Cantera, a volcanic rock commonly found in Mexico and an appropriate choice for this Southern California Mission-style home.

▲ A SET OF CURVING STONE STAIRS provides a graceful entrance to a stone terrace situated at the heart of this small suburban yard. Along with their intrinsic natural beauty, stone stairs feel more solid underfoot, require less maintenance, and last longer than wooden exterior stairs.

▲ BLOCK WALLS VENEERED with slate cut to bricklike size frame the stairs and walkway—also veneered with slate—leading to this Los Angeles home. Chosen for its subtle color variations and unassuming presence, slate has a casual feel that matches the modest dimensions of this home.

Safety First

I F YOU'VE EVER STUMBLED on a flight of uneven stairs, you know that stairway safety is a serious matter. Because stone steps are irregular by nature, they present the potential for serious injury. Here are some ways to make stone staircases safer:

- Make sure riser heights vary by no more than $3/4$ in. (less variance is better).
- Break up long flights of steps with landings at least the width of the steps and about the depth of three treads.
- Provide adequate lighting for nighttime use.
- Make sure treads are stable and securely supported.
- Choose stones with an even surface and coarse, nonslip texture for treads.
- Provide a handrail.

◄ SECURELY MORTARED to a sturdy concrete base, these 5-ft.-wide Shenandoah flagstone steps gracefully link the upper and lower terraces of this San Francisco Bay–area home together while inviting further exploration of the gardens surrounding the house.

INFORMAL STEPS

▲ FOR SAFETY'S SAKE, it's important that stone steps have a relatively smooth and slip-resistant tread surface, even when they are part of a rustic woodland path. Though often overlooked, a secure handrail built in a style to match the setting makes all stairs safer.

◄ ▲ STEPS SERVE AS TRANSITIONAL ELEMENTS that help link separate spaces together. For example, the natural change in elevation and the use of stone in the entry courtyard of this Seattle home (above) signals both a change in grade and a change from public to private space. Elsewhere in the garden, two brick terraces that look similar but that serve different functions are separated—and linked—by a few stone steps, a transition highlighted by plantings that frame the passageway (left).

◄ INTENDED MORE to aid in garden maintenance rather than act as a thoroughfare, a set of simple flagstone steps brings a sense of order to these lushly overflowing planting beds and provides dry footing in the heart of the garden.

Calculating the Number of Steps

To DETERMINE THE NUMBER OF STEPS needed for a set of stairs, you'll first need to measure the slope's rise, which is simply the change in vertical elevation from bottom (Point A) to top (Point B). You can do this by laying a long 2x4 or other straightedge on the ground at the top of the slope, using a carpenter's level to make sure the 2x4 is perfectly horizontal, then measuring the rise with a tape measure.

You'll also need to determine the slope's run, which is simply the horizontal distance between points A and B. Steep slopes will have a shorter run, while gentle slopes will have longer runs. To find the run, simply measure the horizontal distance from where you want your stairs to start to where they'll end.

Divide the rise by the projected height of your riser to tentatively arrive at the number of steps you'll need.

For example, a slope with a rise of 30 in. will require six 5-in.-high steps. If the treads are 15 in. deep, those six steps will cover a run of 90 in. Adjust the height of your riser and depth of your tread so that the stairs are neither too steep nor too shallow, perhaps setting a few stones in place to get a sense of how the stairs will feel.

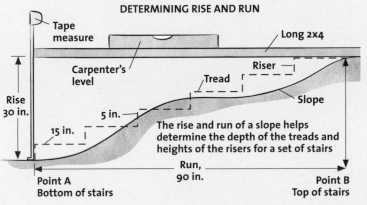

DETERMINING RISE AND RUN

Tape measure
Long 2x4
Carpenter's level
Riser
Tread
Rise 30 in.
5 in.
Slope
15 in.
The rise and run of a slope helps determine the depth of the treads and heights of the risers for a set of stairs
Run, 90 in.
Point A Bottom of stairs
Point B Top of stairs

Risers and Treads

BECAUSE YOUR FEET ARE VERY SENSITIVE to even a slight difference in the height of one step compared to another, risers (the vertical distance between steps) should be consistently sized, usually between 4 in. and 8 in., and should vary in height by no more than 3/4 in. Treads (the horizontal part of the step) should measure at least 12 in. deep and depending on the slope and design of the stairs, can be much wider. A good formula for calculating properly proportioned steps is (Riser x 2) + tread depth = 25 in. to 27 in.

A good riser height for exterior stairs is 5 in., which would result in an ideal tread width of 15 in. to 17 in. Deeper treads encourage a leisurely pace, while shallower treads dictate a no-nonsense ascent or descent. In general, exterior stairs have shallower risers and deeper treads than interior stairs.

Suitable tread stone should have an even surface but shouldn't be so smooth that it would become dangerously slippery when wet. If supported by stone risers, treads can be as thin as 2 in. or so, but keep in mind that thicker, heavier stones will be more stable if the steps aren't mortared.

▲ LARGE STONES STEP UP THE SIDE of a moss-covered slope, creating a serene pathway through this Missouri woodland retreat. Keep in mind that moss, which thrives in moist, shaded sites and can grow on just about anything, including rock, can be slippery when wet.

▲ NATIVE FIELDSTONE SLABS, stacked to create flights of informal steps and a series of stone planters, also function as retaining walls on this sloped site. Night lighting provided by strategically placed low-voltage lighting fixtures makes these steps safer after sundown.

◄ WHILE STONE SLAB TREADS offer a solid and secure walking surface, steps can also be built with smaller stones, which are lighter and easier to handle. Grass growing between the individual stones making up these treads helps the steps blend into the landscape.

◄ ▼ STONE STEPS PROVIDE A PERFECT VENUE for a variety of plantings. Creepers such as thyme and Corsican mint don't grow very high, making them a good choice to fill in between stepping stones (left) while larger, more dramatic plants can be planted along the edges (below).

Terraces, Patios, and Garden Spaces

Carpetlike lawns once ruled the American landscape. Now, though, homeowners in both warm and cold climates are discovering ways to extend living spaces out into their yards, creating outdoor areas—for dining, gardening, or simply relaxing—that family and friends can enjoy together. Stone is an ideal all-season material for these spaces, offering a durable and beautiful surface that requires little or no maintenance.

All around the outside of the house, stone can be used to create a variety of inviting spaces that echo the architectural style of your home. Designs featuring smooth, cut stones laid in tight patterns provide an elegant look as well as a smooth, secure surface for furniture and guests. Natural stones with irregular shapes and textures can be used to complement or emphasize a more rustic surrounding environment. And, of course, patterns, colors, textures, and styles can be mixed and matched to lend just the right touch to your landscape design, whether your tastes tend toward the formal or the informal and whether your special outdoor place is just outside the door or tucked away in your own secret garden.

◄ SURROUNDED BY PERIWINKLE AND HOSTAS, these circular sitting areas are paved with cut bluestone and connected with bluestone stepping stones, a unifying theme that's echoed by the bluestone capping the stone wall. The tall cedar hedge that borders this suburban backyard helps create a sense of privacy.

Sitting Places

From intimate nooks tucked into garden corners to spacious patios with commanding vistas, outdoor sitting areas benefit from various types of enclosures to make them comfortable. The sky may be the ceiling, but boundaries—adjacent house walls, a picket fence, a dense hedge, or a stone wall—will help make your space feel both private and sheltering. While a sitting place should benefit from the sun, think too about protective shade, whether by a natural tree canopy, an arbor, or simply an umbrella or awning. You'll also want to consider siting your sitting area so that it takes advantage of the views and sounds of your property. Ultimately, the right combination of choices will provide you with a stylish and comfortable outdoor refuge and a favorite place to relax and enjoy time with family and friends.

▼ PIECED TOGETHER LIKE A JIGSAW PUZZLE, this fieldstone terrace overlooks one of the numerous salt ponds that dot the island of Martha's Vineyard off the Massachusetts coast. Plants in the crevices between stones and the terrace's naturally irregular edge and low profile help it meld into the landscape.

▲ TIRED OF THE ENDLESS CYCLE of lawn and flower-bed maintenance during the long, hot Atlanta summers, these homeowners chose a landscape design that features fieldstone sitting areas and walkways and a small pond (top and above). The naturalistic approach to garden design emphasizes native plants chosen to reflect the natural cycles of different types of Southeast ecosystems, while the local fieldstone presents a practical, rustically textured walking surface.

▲ **THE IRREGULAR SURFACE** of a fieldstone terrace provides less stability than smooth, cut-stone pavers for patio furniture, yet the relaxed look is a perfect match for this country home, especially when combined with a rustic twig arbor.

▲ A CIVILIZED OASIS SURROUNDED by nature, this dining terrace is built with bluestone pavers that have a thermal finish, where the stone has been flame-treated to create a slightly pebbled, nonslip surface. In contrast, the lichen-covered fieldstone stepping stones leading up to the terrace have rough texture and an aged patina (top). The "snowflake" terrace design (above) was inspired by a traditional Scandinavian sweater pattern, reflecting the Norwegian heritage of the homeowner.

▲ HISTORIC SPANISH AND PORTUGUESE PLAZAS and sidewalks were sometimes paved with pebbles, a practice that inspires contemporary designers to create elaborate mosaics out of river rock, pebbles, marbles, and other materials set in mortar. This modified classic Persian carpet design represents the creation of the universe.

◄ MEASURING JUST A FEW square feet, this small terrace offers a comfortable spot for quiet conversation. Large Mexican sandstone flagstones set in mortar provide a smooth, secure surface for potted plants and furniture, and a slightly rustic look that matches the relaxed atmosphere of the surrounding gardens.

Plants for Patios

L IKE PATHWAYS, PATIOS PRESENT a perfect opportunity to marry the hard and enduring qualities of stone with the ephemeral beauty of plantings. Depending on how formal or how casual you want your landscape to look, you can use a number of different planting strategies. For example, to give a more informal quality to a patio composed of square cut stone, leave a little more space between the pavers, fill the spaces with a sand/loam mixture instead of mortar, and plant a low ground cover. Try to leave at least 2 in. of room between stones so that the roots won't dry out. If your patio is composed of fieldstone or flagstone, using the same strategy will help soften the look of the stone and reinforce a casual feel (right). To keep your space looking organized instead of overgrown, limit these types of plantings to one or two species.

Another strategy is to actually remove the occasional paver or stone and create a planting pocket. In this case, larger plants can be used to create small focal points in your terrace. An advantage to this technique is that you can experiment with different plant combinations and locations from year to year.

◄ LOW GROUND COVERS, such as this Corsican mint, can be planted between the dry-laid stones of both flagstone and paver patios, helping to soften the look of the stone and introduce a more casual atmosphere to the terrace.

▲ SHADED FROM THE HOT LATE-AFTERNOON SUN, the bluestone patio of this Maine cottage enjoys a sunny southeastern exposure, making cool coastal mornings feel just a little warmer. Though not local, the large bluestone flagstones coordinate well with the local granite used for the patio's steps and foundation.

▲ CRUSHED STONE AND OTHER AGGREGATES offer a versatile walking surface, but if you're considering an aggregate for a sitting area, keep in mind that most patio furniture sits more steadily on a smooth surface, such as the large cast-concrete pavers used in this backyard courtyard.

▲ THOUGH THE SALTWATER VIEWS from this large patio are expansive, the low, curving stone wall and planting bed borders keep this sitting area from feeling too exposed. Colored concrete pavers set in stack bond and herringbone patterns mimic the curved design of the surrounding landscaped gardens.

Shopping for Patio Stone

WHERE SHOULD YOU GO TO FIND just the right paving material for your patio? You can start at your local home improvement center, where you're likely to find a fairly good selection of concrete pavers and possibly a limited selection of stone. Or try a well-stocked gardening center, which should offer various types of stone and pavers. For the best selection, be prepared to take a road trip (or two) to nearby stoneyards. Here you'll find the broadest offering of local stone (usually the best for your project) and sometimes examples of more exotic and salvaged stones as well.

▲ SUNNY AND PRIVATE, the charming master bedroom terrace of this oceanfront home on Martha's Vineyard is made with beach cobble collected from the nearby shoreline. A winding path built with large, irregular fieldstone connects the terrace to the beach.

Dining Places

THERE'S NO RULE THAT STATES that an intimate dining area can't be carved out of a secluded corner of your garden. If you're blessed with a magnificent vista from one of the far reaches of your property, you may want to situate a table and chairs there to take advantage of the view while enjoying a picnic lunch. But for convenience, most outdoor dining areas are located adjacent to the house and near the kitchen. For any outdoor space that is close to the house, consider relating one to the other using similar materials, furnishings, or styles. For example, a cut-stone floor could be installed in a style that echoes an indoor tile floor. Also, you'll need space for accommodating a dining set and traffic; in fact, it's wise to scale all outdoor spaces larger than their interior counterparts, if possible, to keep them in proportion with your home's exterior dimensions.

▶ RELATIVELY INEXPENSIVE AND EASY to install, landscape aggregates such as gravel, crushed stone, and pebbles are equally at home in sitting areas and along walkways. Small-sized aggregates—from 3/8 in. to 1/2 in. in diameter—will offer better stability under furniture and feet than larger ones.

▲ THOUGH THIS CAST-CONCRETE DINING SET is rigidly geometric, the casual fieldstone patio underneath, groundcover growing in the crevices between the stones, and lush surrounding gardens visually soften its hard surfaces and bring informality to the space.

▲ IRISH MOSS GROWS BETWEEN the petal-shaped flagstones of this Cape Cod patio, creating a contrast that emphasizes the stone's light color and organic shapes. Quarried from an ancient lake bed, the stone has a uniquely grooved, wavelike surface texture.

Beyond Stone: Brick and Concrete Pavers

AS FAR AS LANDSCAPE SURFACING MATERIALS GO, **there is a wide range of stonelike options for building terraces and patios. Concrete pavers offer probably the widest range of shapes, sizes, styles, and colors of any hardscaping material, and generally at reasonable cost. Shapes range from simple squares and rectangles to interesting interlocking designs, while their color palette—though tending toward earthtones—is virtually unlimited. Surface textures can vary from rough to smooth, with tumbled and preweathered finishes available to give them the look of old stone (photos far right).**

Brick is another traditional choice, but keep in mind that there are many different types of bricks. Those intended specifically for exterior use—called paver bricks—are harder and less likely to absorb moisture than structural bricks, which aren't intended for exposure to weather. Most paver bricks have a uniform texture and color, and while they are available in different sizes and finishes, tend to have a commercial look. A few manufacturers offer antique-looking paver bricks with a tumbled finish that would look right at home in a cottage garden. Don't rule out old, salvaged bricks, regardless of their source; those that wear out over time are generally easy to replace.

▲ PERHAPS THE MOST economical paving material, brick is available in a limited range of colors and in various shapes, sizes, and finishes. Intended for exterior use, paver bricks can be molded (top) or extruded (bottom), and are also available with a tumbled finish (second from bottom). Unlike most antique building materials, you won't pay a premium for most salvaged bricks (second from top), though they may not be ideally suited for use on a patio.

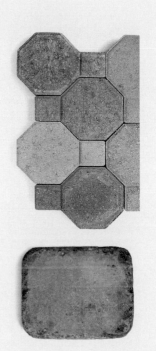

▲ AN ECONOMICAL hardscaping choice, concrete pavers are available in a wide range of styles, colors, sizes, and shapes. Interlocking pavers are designed to fit closely together (top) and can be used to create a cobbled courtyard appearance, while some concrete pavers are also available with a tumbled finish that resembles natural stone (bottom).

▲ ONCE PART OF A 1940s CALIFORNIA COTTAGE that burned down, a brick fireplace is now the focal point of this elegant garden "dining room." The slate tile floor's rich texture and warm color compliments the redwood pergola, while oak trees and potted cyprus further define the room's edges.

▲ OVERLOOKING THE PACIFIC OCEAN, this mortared flagstone terrace provides a stable, level surface for furniture. Low plantings provide a natural border without blocking the view, while the stonework creates a secure environment that feels firmly anchored to the ground in spite of the dramatic vista.

▶ PART OF A THREE-SECTION OUTDOOR ROOM flanking a 1940s West Hollywood home, this outdoor dining area features a floor of antique limestone pavers. A 12-ft.-high ficus hedge wall screens the spaces, while a sculpture of Icarus rises up out of a bronze-trimmed pool filled with water lilies.

▲ **BY EMBEDDING VARIOUS SIZES**, colors, and types of stone and other aggregates into mortar, you can incorporate permanent designs and patterns into the surface of your patio. Made with contrasting stones set in a tinted mortar, the stylized sun at this dining area's entrance shines daily.

▲ TIGHTLY AND UNIFORMLY LAID stone pavers in a range of shades compliment the tropical colors and relaxed though ordered look of this intimate dining area.

▲ SITUATED JUST SLIGHTLY off the flagstone path, this informal eating area is located far enough away from the house to turn a simple meal into a romantic outing. Sunlight splashes down through the trees, which also provide shade, and gardens offer plenty of privacy.

▲ LARGE BLUESTONE PAVERS surrounded by a contrasting border of brick further define the sitting area created by flowering shrubs and hedges in this Nantucket garden.

▲ LIMESTONE PAVERS RANGING IN SIZE from 6 in. by 6 in. to 16 in. by 16 in. line the floor of this Los Angeles-area dining terrace. The floor's ordered yet informal look makes for an easy transition into the garden spaces around the house.

◀ LOOKING LIKE A NATURAL EXTENSION of the house, the cut-stone pavers of this patio match the hue of the home's clapboard siding. The generously sized space offers plenty of room for a dining set and can easily accommodate traffic through and around the area.

Outdoor Rooms

I N THE ARID COUNTRIES SURROUNDING THE MEDITERRANEAN, homes are often organized around a central courtyard. Embellished with fountains, hearths, and gardens, these outdoor living rooms are at the focal point of family and social life. While the option of year-round outdoor living isn't always available in the wide-ranging American climate, the idea of a roomlike outdoor space that can be enjoyed in the warmer months is finding a wider audience all across the country. A sense of enclosure—both physical and psychological—is essential for these spaces, including an arrangement of man-made or natural walls or screens that provide privacy while allowing just the right amount of air movement so that the space is neither too hot nor too cold. Shelter or shade overhead is optional, depending on the climate.

▲ THOUGH CUT INTO 12-IN. SQUARE TILES and laid in a regular pattern, the variegated colors that are characteristic of Indian slate give this floor a warm texture that provides an organic contrast to the more formal columns and trellis of this penthouse pergola.

▶ SHADED BY A FORMAL TRELLIS and conveniently located near the pool, this versatile outdoor room offers a comfortable setting for conversations, meals, and enjoying a view of the water. The randomly sized, cut-bluestone pavers offer smooth, secure footing and just the right touch of informality.

A Well-Designed Courtyard

THOUGH USUALLY ASSOCIATED WITH WARM, sunny locations, a properly designed courtyard that takes optimum advantage of its site can provide nearly year-round use in a variety of climates. Located in Portland, Oregon, this courtyard has a subtropical feel thanks to its east-southeast exposure (which maximizes sun exposure without overheating the space) and the shelter offered by two walls of the house. The remaining two sides of the courtyard are enclosed by cinder block walls, which give the space privacy and block the wind. The microclimate created by this arrangement of exposure and enclosure is warm enough to support the tropical plants that screen the cinder block walls. In warm climates, a courtyard's sun exposure should be minimized, while in cold climates it should be maximized.

While courtyards can be paved with a wide variety of materials, including stone and brick, this one is covered with three types of concrete pavers. Varying in color, texture, and size, these pavers bring welcome color to the garden, especially during Portland's wet, rainy winters. Set on the diagonal in sand, individual pavers can be periodically replaced or removed to accommodate a temporary planting.

▶ SUPPORTED BY A 6-FT. BY 12-FT. acid-washed concrete basin, this cast-iron fountain stands 12 ft. tall and offers a dramatic focal point that helps unify the design of this courtyard garden.

▲ ENCLOSED ON ALL FOUR SIDES, this Portland, Oregon, courtyard is warm enough to support a variety of subtropical plants. A colonnade of concrete columns around the interior of the courtyard helps define the space and create an area for plantings, while a floor of large and small pavers in contrasting colors contributes an interesting visual texture.

▲ JUST A FEW STEPS outside the door, this intimate patio has been carved out of a hillside that's held in place with a distinctive retaining wall laid in a random ashlar pattern. The stone's texture and light coloration add to the feminine quality of the space.

▲ A COLLAGE OF BRICK AND STONE surrounded by ivy-covered walls, this courtyard floor has the aura of antiquity. The rectangular brick grid brings a subtle sense of order to the randomly sized and patterned stonework and helps define the separate functions served by the "room."

▶ SET IN A GROVE OF TREES and announced by a pergola, this small woodland terrace offers a not too rustic setting for communing with nature. The low profile and fieldstone construction help it blend unobtrusively into the landscape.

▲ LAID IN A RUNNING BOND PATTERN, the brick paver floor of this Santa Fe pavilion makes the transition between indoor and outdoor spaces an easy one while complementing the rusty hues of the moss rock wall and mantle over the fireplace.

▲ A BEAUTIFUL CONTRAST to the symmetry of the exposed roof framing above, the random pattern of this flagstone floor adds to the relaxed atmosphere of this outdoor living room. The floor's tightly laid, neutral, grey-colored stones have an understated presence that helps direct attention toward the fireplace.

◀ LOCATED OVER 100 FT. from the main house, this outdoor room offers a quiet getaway. The crushed granite floor deadens footfalls, while the veneered stone wall offers plenty of informal seating, both on the wall itself and on stone slabs cantilevered out from the higher privacy wall.

Garden Paths and Floors

MANY WOULD ARGUE THAT A GARDEN WITHOUT STONE is like a garden without plantings. Stone provides an enduring framework for the lush but transient beauty of ground covers, flowers, herbs and grasses, and shrubs and trees. There are, of course, numerous creative possibilities for using stone in the garden, from walls and borders to water structures and decorative work. But underfoot is where you can really take advantage of the best practical and decorative qualities of stone. Used simply and sparingly—a small flagstone terrace tucked into a garden corner, for example—stone can produce a subtle enhancement, but can also be employed for a more complex or dramatic effect. A network of paths and patios composed of both cut and natural stone, for example, can work to unify a garden landscape. Whether formal or informal, stone in the garden is a natural fit.

▲ NEARLY OVERGROWN WITH GROUND COVER and interspersed with planting pockets, this rustic flagstone terrace offers a woodsy welcome to this Atlanta home. Potted plantings create a focal point and can be used as such in any landscape.

▼ TUCKED WITHIN THE BOUNDARIES of an old, rubble-wall barn foundation, this sunken garden offers both shelter from the breeze and terrific views of the surrounding landscape. The sitting area is paved with large flagstones that preserve the "as-found" look.

▶ VERSATILE AS WELL AS BEAUTIFUL, stone is also well suited for urban settings. Here grey granite curbs help frame the formal planting beds of this city garden, and keep loose stone pathways from migrating into planted areas.

▲▶ **FLANKED BY RAISED BEDS** and stone retaining walls, this garden pathway (left) steps slowly up toward a small, ancient-looking hillside terrace (above). The retaining walls were built with stone hauled from an abandoned hunting lodge, while the terrace is paved with reclaimed stone pavers from the streets of Atlanta. Creepers growing between the pavers add to the antiquated look of this 100-year-old Georgia log cabin (top).

▲ PLANTED ON A KNOLL, this rock garden offers a naturalistic counterpoint to a patio made with interlocking concrete pavers. When creating a rock garden, use a single type of stone, bury large rocks by at least a third, and position smaller rocks after large rocks are in place.

▲ THOUGH ALL LOADS OF STONE will inevitably include a certain percentage that is unsuitable for paving or walls, the odd-size remainders can be turned into an asset. Here, a loosely constructed sculpture made with irregularly shaped native fieldstone is the focal point of this small Vermont garden.

▼ FILLED WITH AN ECLECTIC MIX of herbs surrounding a central bed of annuals, this Texas garden is arranged in a maze-like circle to encourage exploration, and features paths of crushed granite and planting beds bordered by blocks of native Texas limestone.

A Backyard Oasis

USING A LITTLE INGENUITY **and the right combination of stone and plantings, it's possible to** transform even a small, urban backyard into a tranquil, leafy refuge. This is exactly what garden designer Verle Lessig did with the 25-ft. by 50-ft. backyard of his Chicago-area home. To make the space feel secluded, Lessig erected a 6-ft. fence (the tallest allowed by local zoning regulations) around the perimeter of the yard, then excavated down a foot to create a sunken patio. He then dug a 6-ft. by 12-ft. pond, using the excess soil to create berms that slope up toward the surrounding fence. Artificial boulders—chosen to match the color and texture of the hand-picked flagstones that pave the patio—form a waterfall and stream that empty into the pond. The splashing water creates a pleasing, natural sound while simultaneously drowning out urban noise. Flowers, plants, shrubs, and trees complete the picture, screening the fence with lush greenery, enhancing the privacy of the space, and transporting family and friends to a magical paradise.

▶ WHEN VIEWED FROM GROUND LEVEL (right), this flagstone patio and adjoining pond have a rural feel, but the view from this Chicago area home's second-story window (top right) reveals how the creative use of stone and plantings helped transform this tiny urban backyard into a peaceful retreat. The flagstones used for the patio were chosen for their rustic color and texture, and their irregular shapes were carefully laid out to create a pleasing pattern.

Poolside Spaces

BECAUSE OF THE IMPRESSIVE PHYSICAL DIMENSIONS of most swimming pools, they are a dominating feature in any landscape. A good landscaping plan can help to harmonize a pool with its surroundings while creating a safe and comfortable environment, recognizing all the while that most of the action associated with a pool takes place around it rather than in it. This is where stone is really in its element, playing important aesthetic and functional roles. When placed around the deck of a pool, stone beautifully frames the water's ever-changing surface. The wide variety of available stones allows you to choose a durable and slip-resistant surface, be it formal or informal. Stone walls are a natural choice for enclosing poolside spaces, while stone walkways can be used to connect them to other parts of your property. Use boulders and rocks to add a naturally dramatic element to the area.

▶ **CLIMBING ROSES THRIVE** in the sunny, sheltered space created by the native New England fieldstone walls that buffer this pool from Cape Cod's harsh ocean environment. The pool's bluestone terrace paving is echoed by the bluestone caps on the walls and pillars.

◄ SURROUNDED BY WALLS OF STACKED, broken concrete, this sunken pool in California's West Hollywood hills is paved with tumbled concrete pavers set in a basketweave pattern. Steps of broken concrete lead down to the pool area.

► LIKE THE MATCHING CHIMNEY, the fieldstone wall enclosing this pool area was built with mortar (cleverly concealed with tucked joints) for strength. The accompanying coping and paving—quarried nearby from weathered slabs of granite—match the look of the large boulder that anchors the wall.

Paver Patterns

BECAUSE MODULAR PAVERS—SUCH AS BRICK, CONCRETE, AND SOME TYPES OF COBBLESTONES—are produced in uniform sizes and shapes, they can be installed in a variety of patterns. These patterns will affect the look of your patio or terrace, the method and degree of difficulty of the installation, and even the specific type of paver that you can use. Some of the most popular modular paver patterns include the following:

■ Stack bond—Sometimes called "Jack-on-Jack," this is the simplest to install and may not require any cuts at all.

■ Running bond—When properly spaced, this easy-to-install pattern requires only a half-cut paver every other row.

■ Herringbone—This pattern can be installed in either a straight or angled orientation. Pavers used for herringbone patterns need to be sized precisely, with their widths equal to half their lengths.

■ Basketweave—Another easy pattern to install, this doesn't require many cuts, but does require pavers that are exactly twice as long as they are wide.

■ Pinwheel—This pattern creates an interesting optical effect and requires one half-size paver for every five full-size pavers (again, pavers must be twice as long as they are wide).

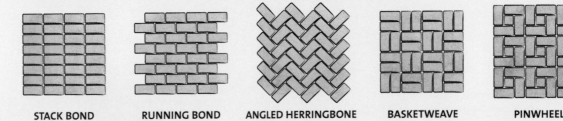

STACK BOND   RUNNING BOND   ANGLED HERRINGBONE   BASKETWEAVE   PINWHEEL

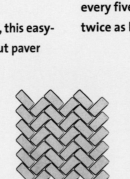

◀ ▲ THREE WALLS—A SCULPTURAL CONCRETE retaining wall, a new fieldstone seatwall, and a vintage "lace" wall built long ago from irregular native stone—surround this pool on Martha's Vineyard (left). Standing 4 ft. high off the ground around the outside of the pool, the seatwall meets local pool enclosure code requirements. The lighter-colored Wisconsin limestone paving around the pool creates an evenly textured contrast that's also cooler underfoot than darker-colored paving materials might be (above).

▶ A STEPPING-STONE PATH made with New Hampshire schist leads up to a poolside patio paved with Pennsylvania bluestone. The path and patio stones were chosen to match the color and texture of the old stone walls that surround this rural Vermont property.

▲ THOUGH THE ARCHITECTURE is decidedly contemporary, the flagstone and aggregate deck around this pool provides more texture and warmth than would a concrete deck. Quarried in Mariposa, California, the Yosemite black slate flagstones are notable for their gold flecking and the rich color and texture variations.

◄ A FLAGSTONE TERRACE, stone steps, and fieldstone retaining walls help create a relaxed atmosphere around this New England pool.

Walls

Walls bring order to the natural landscape. Useful for physically defining property boundaries, they also serve to delineate areas that have different characters—a pool from a lawn, for example, or a driveway from a nearby garden. Freestanding walls can be used to influence traffic patterns, blocking access on the one hand while directing people—via gates, arches, or steps—on the other. On hilly terrain, retaining walls help hold back the soil to create level places for patios and gardens. Of course, a masonry wall can be used to create a sense of privacy and, with the proper exposure, can produce its own microclimate, absorbing the sun's warmth while blocking chilling winds.

Stone is a logical and natural choice for walls. It is durable and low-maintenance and, though more expensive than other wall-building materials—such as wood or metal fencing—it will far outlast them all. Stone walls can be designed to suit any style of landscape, from rigidly formal to ruggedly natural. Whether your walls are built from stone gathered on the site or from rock quarried in a far-off location, they'll give your landscape a unique character that will endure for generations to come.

◄ **WHETHER DRY-LAID OR BUILT** with mortar, stone walls add a distinctive character to the landscape. This freestanding dry-laid wall separates a garden from an adjacent lawn, while built-in planting pockets blur the transition between one area and the other.

Dry Stone Walls

IN SOME PARTS OF THE COUNTRY, STONE WALLS ARE A NATURAL part of the landscape, looking as though they've been in place for centuries. In fact, in many cases they have: Created by early farmers as they cleared the land of rocks and piled them off to the sides, some of these informal walls have survived into the 21st century, even though the fields they once bordered may have long since reverted back to forest. What was once a practical necessity has evolved into a craft, and now a well-made dry stone wall is much treasured for its natural look and traditional feel. Elegant and simple at the same time, dry stone walls—which rely only on gravity, friction, and the skill of the builder to stay together—can be built as decorative freestanding versions or functional retaining types that will help define and enhance your landscape.

◀ ▲ **PART OF THE RENOVATION** of this old Maine farm involved stabilizing an 1897 barn, lifting it off its original rubble fieldstone foundation and placing it onto a new poured concrete foundation. The old stones were recycled and used to build both the dry stacked freestanding wall in the foreground and the retaining wall that supports the circular patio in the background (above).

◄ DRY STACKED RETAINING WALLS can be built with a variety of stone types; the most commonly used include limestone, granite, and sandstone. The uniform color and rectangular shapes of the stones in this retaining wall give it an even texture and a formal, brick-like quality.

▼ A RICHLY TEXTURED, organic composition of smoothly rounded stones, this retaining wall nicely complements the Arts-and-Crafts style of this Ventura, California, home, which was designed by Henry Greene and built in 1924.

FREESTANDING WALLS

▲ ONCE BUILT AS A PRACTICAL MATTER while clearing fields of stones for plowing and to define property boundaries, stone walls still resonate with agricultural tradition. Built with native fieldstone, this long wall creates a dramatic sight line in this pastoral landscape.

▲ CAREFULLY FITTED JOINTS emphasize the range of sizes, shapes, and shadings of the individual stones used to build this short section of a nearly 1,000-ft.-long wall, made from a combination of local stone and stone brought to Martha's Vineyard from Maine and New Hampshire.

▲ BECAUSE A DRY STONE WALL doesn't have a rigid concrete foundation, it remains flexible and can absorb the soil movement caused by freeze/thaw cycles and tree root growth. If a section of wall comes tumbling down, the stones can be easily repositioned.

▲ STONE WALLS CAN BE USED to define different areas; here, a low wall of New England fieldstone separates a parking area and garage from a garden. It also creates a backdrop to a colorful perennial border and helps screen the view of cars from the house.

A Dry Stone Wall Primer

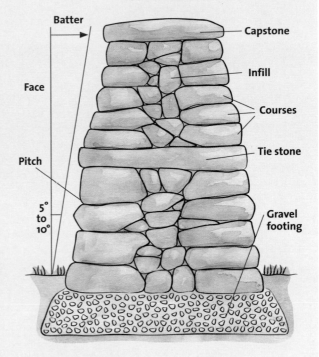

A DRY STONE WALL

B ECAUSE DRY STONE WALLS HAVE historically been built with native stone, it's best to follow that tradition if you're planning one for your property. Choose local stones, or stones that are similar to local ones in color and texture; if there are existing walls nearby, try to match their scale and appearance. Good stones for building dry walls have relatively flat faces and at least two angled edges, and include limestones, sandstones, and granites.

A dry stone wall doesn't require a concrete foundation, but it should rest on a firm footing and seem to grow out of the ground rather than sit on top of it. Most dry stone wallers (as opposed to stonemasons, who work primarily with stone and mortar) dig a trench, fill it with 1-in. of gravel to within 6 in. of ground level, and then begin building the stone wall using the largest stones for base stones. As they lay up the courses of the wall, they remember this simple rule: two stones over one stone, one stone over two stones. A well-proportioned stone wall measures 2 ft. wide by 3 ft. high, or about 3 ft. wide by 4 ft. high.

Labels on diagram: Batter, Face, Pitch, 5° to 10°, Capstone, Infill, Courses, Tie stone, Gravel footing

◄ EVEN THE MOST INFORMAL, casually stacked stone wall has a charming and useful presence when properly sited. The low wall that defines the border between this lawn and garden lends structure to the landscape, even after the brilliant colors of the garden have faded.

RETAINING WALLS

▲ STONE STILES WERE ONCE BUILT into some farm walls as an alternative to a gate, providing a way for people—but not animals—to get to the other side of a wall. Here they play a more decorative role in this attractive retaining wall.

▲ THOUGH LOCATED in the San Francisco Bay area, moss, planting pockets, and irregularly shaped stone help this retaining wall capture the look and feel of an antique Irish wall. Built with limestone quarried in the midwestern United States, its design reflects the homeowner's Celtic heritage.

▲ RAISED PLANTING BEDS placed over rock crevices and filled with additional soil make it easier to garden on a rocky site. These informal retaining walls of layered flat stones help hold the soil in place and provide structure for the planting beds.

Planting Pockets

WHILE A STONE WALL CAN SERVE as a dramatic background for flowers and other plantings, it's also possible to transform a stone wall into a garden. Planting pockets—intentional small gaps and crevices between individual stones that are filled with garden soil—offer a perfect habitat for a wide range of plants in stone walls. Because stone moderates the temperature of the soil, retaining the warmth of the sun in winter months and cooling the soil in hot weather, plants generally thrive in their pockets. Stone also helps soil retain moisture in dry weather, while a stone wall readily drains away excess water during rainy weather.

Planting pockets can be successfully created in freestanding walls, but retaining walls generally offer a better environment for plants. The soil being held back by the stone acts as a moisture "bank," supplying water to the plants and giving roots ample room to grow. Plants that do well in pockets include those with minimal root systems, such as hens and chicks; small creeping plants like creeping thyme; and hardy perennials, such as the many varieties of sedum.

▶ EVEN A FREESTANDING STONE WALL with tightly fitted joints has room for planting pockets. Also known as stonecrop, this assortment of creeping sedums thrives in marginal, well-drained soil. They require sunshine but otherwise minimal maintenance.

▲ LIKE A JIGSAW PUZZLE, this retaining wall is knitted together with tightly fitting joints, a feature that is emphasized by the unusually broad variety of stones used in its construction. The snake ornament adds a playful touch to the formal composition.

▲ BESIDES LEVELING A SLOPED SITE and helping to control erosion, a retaining wall can play host to a wide variety of plantings, including fragrant herbs such as rosemary and thyme.

Batter and Pitch

BATTER (SOMETIMES CALLED THRUST) is the angle that a wall's face leans back from the vertical. Batter concentrates pressure toward the middle of a freestanding wall (both faces slant inward) and helps a retaining wall resist soil pressure; it typically measures between 5 and 10 degrees. All walls should taper back 2 in. for each foot of height (a 1-to-6 ratio).

Pitch is the angle that individual stones should be set within the wall. When stones slope back toward the wall's center, their pitch helps reinforce the batter and resist the force of rainwater flowing over the face.

▲ THIS 1926 MAINE SUMMER COTTAGE was picked up and moved 110 ft. back from the water before being renovated for year-round living. A series of local granite retaining walls that step down toward the waterfront to create grassy terraces was then added.

► A DRY-LAID RETAINING WALL built with a local schist (a layered, coarse-grained rock) creates level planting areas and lawn spaces and helps root this Vermont home into the surrounding landscape. The stepping-stone paths and steps leading up to the house are built with the same schist.

"Tools of the Trade" Retaining Wall

G IVEN A TRACTABLE CLIENT (HERSELF), free design reign, and an ample supply of surplus stone, what kind of wall would a landscaper build? The answer for Vermont landscaper Andrea Morgante is this delightful "Tools of the Trade" dry-laid stone retaining wall. A state sidewalk improvement project gave Morgante the opportunity to put a building yard full of leftover stone, and some limestone taken from a ridge behind her house, to use. As Morgante explains, "There's a geological mixture of stones in the wall, something that I would never normally suggest. But the price was right and I planned on covering the wall with vines if the stone combinations didn't work out."

Working with her longtime collaborator, the talented mason David "Stoney" Mason, Morgante began incorporating a wheelbarrow, wagon wheel, and various other implements into the wall as a whim, which ultimately grew into a theme for the entire project. Pieces of rebar welded to the back of the old tools help anchor them in place in the wall.

▲ THE OLD FARM IMPLEMENTS and garden tools included in this wall's construction help to graphically represent the builder's landscaping business. Lengths of rebar welded to the back of the tools and held in place by the dry stacked stone help to secure them and prevent theft.

◄ THIS WHIMSICAL RETAINING WALL was created with a geological mix of surplus stone and a variety of vintage landscaping tools. The dry-stacked wall's time-worn materials and unique design minimize the visual impact of the new sidewalk on this old Vermont home.

Mortared Walls

WHILE DRY STONE WALLS RELY ON FRICTION and gravity to hold together, wet-laid walls rely on the binding strength of mortar, a mixture of portland cement, sand, and lime. Because mortared walls don't have the inherent flexibility of dry walls, they require a more substantial foundation to prevent settling and cracking. In some situations, a gravel footing is needed to provide adequate strength, but for most mortared walls a concrete footing poured below frost level is required. Once the footing is in place, a mortared wall is actually easier to build than a dry wall because gaps between the stones are filled with mortar, making stone placement less critical. In addition, a wider variety of stones can be used in a mortared wall and a wider range of wall styles can be built—from formal retaining walls to relaxed-looking freestanding walls that appear to be dry-laid.

▲ **DESIGNED TO ADD A SCULPTURAL ELEMENT** to the parking court of this rural New England home, this tall native fieldstone wall is mortared for strength and stability. Tucked mortar joints (where mortar is held back from the face of the stone), however, provide a rustic look.

► **BRICK PILLARS AND COPING** incorporated into this mortared stone wall mirror the brick exterior of the nearby house, creating a strong association between architecture and landscape. Planting pockets help soften the stone and brickwork and hint at the gardens beyond.

▲ BUILT WITH A LOCAL STONE called Napa basalt, this mortared seat wall helps define the edge of the lawn while separating a private spa and a master bedroom suite from the more formal public entry to this San Francisco Bay-area home.

◄ BUILDING A STONE WALL with mortar gives you the flexibility to use various types and sizes of stones, including the small, rounded ones that give this gracefully curving wall its distinctive cobbled texture. Because round stones defy close fitting, wide mortar joints fill in the gaps between them.

FREESTANDING WALLS

▶ SMALL, NATIVE FIELDSTONES held together with mortar give this wall an almost delicate presence. A traditional dry-laid wall of the same height would have required a much wider base and more prominent batter (an angling of the sides of the wall away from the vertical).

▲ WHILE THE STONE WALLS framing the gardens beyond have a muted presence, this overgrown arched entryway elevates the sense of anticipation while offering a dramatic invitation to enter and explore. Mortar helps hold the stonework in the pillars and arch together.

▲ THIS FIELDSTONE WALL (bordering a mid-coastal Maine home) is anchored by a glacial "erratic"—a huge boulder left over from the last glacier. Though the wall and matching chimneys are mortared, the joints are tucked for a dry-laid appearance that mimics the traditional local foundations.

◄ THIS LOW STONE WALL is composed of a mixture of Sonoma and Napa Valley fieldstones, two volcanic basalt rocks native to Northern California, where this garden is located. The wall's shapes and hues are a counterpoint to the even texture and muted color of the adjacent flagstone path.

▲ BUILT WITH NATIVE NEW ENGLAND FIELDSTONE, this mortared wall creates a sunny habitat for climbing roses while satisfying a local building code that requires a 4-ft.-high enclosure around swimming pools. Pillars give the enclosure an architectural quality, while blue-stone capstones match the pool terrace paving.

▲ INVITING FAMILY AND GUESTS out into the yard, this curved sitting wall also defines the lawn's edge, adding form to the natural landscape. Echoing the wall's quiet beauty, stones used in the garden bed and beside the wall subtly keep stone a central part of the landscape.

▶ WHETHER YOU LIVE IN A RURAL or a suburban setting, you can frame an entryway with a pair of mortared stone pillars to create the same sense of formality and security offered by extensive stone walls without the expense of actually building them.

Mortared Walls: Two Options

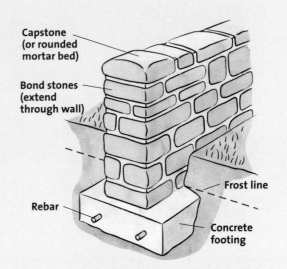

A TRADITIONAL MORTARED WALL OFFERS A NUMBER of advantages over a dry laid wall, including the ability to use virtually any shape or type of stone. In addition, a mortared wall is stronger than one that's dry-laid and doesn't require as much of a batter (or taper) as its counterpart; this means that mortared walls can be tall and narrow.

The one thing that a mortared wall does require that a dry stone wall doesn't is a firm concrete foundation, which can add considerably to labor and building costs. It's possible to get the look of a mortared wall using alternative techniques. In a traditional stone veneer wall, a single layer of stones is supported by a sturdy poured concrete or reinforced block wall. Veneered walls use considerably less stone than conventional mortared walls and can be insulated, making this system suitable for architectural use as well. Of course, stone used in veneer construction needs to be of reasonably uniform thickness.

▲ CONVENTIONAL MORTARED WALL A mortared stone wall's foundation must be adequately sized to support the wall and built below the frost line to prevent cracking. Mortared walls are strongest when vertical joints overlap, while bond stones (also called tie stones) that extend across the width of the wall help to reinforce the wall; they should be laid approximately every third course or so. At the top of the wall, capstones or a mortar bed slightly rounded to shed water help prevent moisture from penetrating the wall, freezing and cracking the mortar joints.

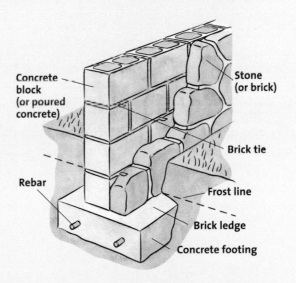

▲ STONE VENEER WALL Used for residential construction as well as for landscaping, this system relies on an inner wall of either poured concrete or concrete block (shown here) to support a single thickness of stone. A brick ledge supports the weight of the stone (or brick), while metal brick ties mortared to the inner wall strengthen the veneer.

RETAINING WALLS

▲ INTENTIONALLY BUILT TO AN 18-IN. HEIGHT to provide comfortable informal seating, this retaining wall is made from an oxidized basalt stone. Broken concrete recycled from an old sidewalk provides backing for the mortared wall, while small river pebbles are fitted into the larger joints between stones.

▲ TERRACED FOR A LOW PROFILE and to create planting areas, this Santa Fe home's retaining walls were first built with concrete block and then veneered with a quarried Arizona sandstone. Low-voltage lighting fixtures have been fitted into cavities built into the block wall (top), a process that is much easier with a veneer system than with a full mortared-stone wall. Full-size capstones (above) help conceal the block construction and give the wall a natural appearance.

▶ THIS RETAINING WALL was built with precast concrete blocks, which are faster and easier to build with than stone. The stucco finish is popular in California, where this wall is located, and the wall is capped with a local volcanic stone to soften its appearance.

▲ A LONG, SERPENTINE RETAINING WALL follows this rural site's natural contours and creates level sitting areas. Built with native fieldstone to match existing farm buildings and stone walls found in New York's Hudson River Valley, the wall provides a local context for the complex of additions to the original 19th-century farmhouse.

▲ SLOPING DOWNWARD TO FOLLOW the contour of the landscape, this fieldstone retaining wall defines the edge of a cottage garden and helps frame the stairway leading up to the house.

▲ BUILDING WITH MORTAR gives you the option of incorporating different design elements in walls, including bricks and rounded stones (left). By tooling the mortar joints, the mortar itself can become part of the design (right).

Modular Retaining Walls

IF YOUR SITE REQUIRES RETAINING WALLS and you like the look of stone—but not the price—you might want to consider one of the many different styles of interlocking concrete blocks that are available. Segmental retaining wall systems made with precast concrete blocks can be found in a wide range of styles, including some that look just like cobblestones and others that are more uniform. While these modular systems cost more than landscaping timbers, they'll last considerably longer. They're self-aligning, so the individual blocks go together easily, and because they require neither a concrete foundation nor mortar to hold them together, segmental retaining wall systems can be built relatively fast. When properly installed with solid footings, good drainage, and sturdy tiebacks to help keep the wall from toppling over, interlocking concrete blocks can be used for building tall retaining walls, though walls over 3 ft. high should be engineered (most retaining walls will also require a building permit). Most interlocking concrete blocks allow you to build curved walls, and some are designed to accommodate stairs, planters, and even integral lighting systems. At around $25 per square foot installed, they cost about half as much as a comparable mortared fieldstone wall.

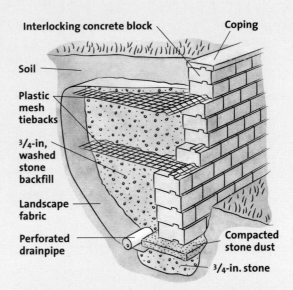

Interlocking concrete block · Coping · Soil · Plastic mesh tiebacks · 3/4-in, washed stone backfill · Landscape fabric · Perforated drainpipe · Compacted stone dust · 3/4-in. stone

▲ A SEGMENTAL RETAINING WALL Interlocking concrete blocks go together quickly and easily without mortar. All retaining walls, regardless of their construction, should have a firm foundation and adequate drainage, and be securely anchored into the slope to prevent the wall from toppling due to pressure from the weight of soil and water.

◄ "MOSS ROCK" IS AN ARIZONA SANDSTONE that has an aged patina. Here it's been used to build a mortared retaining wall that defines the edge of this Santa Fe home's brick paver driveway while serving as a planter for a piñon pine tree.

Nightlighting Your Walls

▲ THE TOP OF A PILLAR or column is an ideal (and traditional) location for an outdoor lighting fixture, serving both a decorative and a practical function. This fixture's height ensures a 360-degree circle of light is cast across a broad area; its translucent lens helps cut glare.

Safety and security are important elements in any landscape lighting plan. A few well-placed lighting fixtures that adequately illuminate paths, entryways, and grade changes can make a big difference in how safe and comfortable your property is to negotiate at night. Because stone walls often flank walkways or enclose an outdoor space, they offer a convenient location for lighting fixtures. While some fixtures are designed to be unobtrusively recessed so that the light source remains hidden, surface-mounted fixtures affixed directly to a stone wall can be used to provide both illumination and a decorative element, and are available in a wide range of styles and finishes.

In addition, many walls are built with pillars that mark the end of a wall section or that frame a passageway through the wall; these offer logical fixture locations. Like the beacon of a lighthouse, pillar-mounted fixtures draw attention to the entry and also help light the way (above). Stone walls can also be illuminated with spotlights located above or below the wall. This kind of effect lighting provides general illumination and emphasizes a wall's texture, adding an element of drama as well as safety to the nightscape.

▲ MOUNTED BELOW EYE LEVEL, these fixtures cast a soft, glare-free light that highlights the texture of the stone wall and illuminates the ground nearby.

▲ **A CAST-STONE DRAGON** stands watch over this mortared retaining wall, which separates the rolling lawns surrounding this Atlanta home from the not-too-wild woods beyond.

Landscaping Features

I f you hike or do a bit of exploring, perhaps along rocky mountain paths, stone-studded creeks, or beaches, you've surely come across a pile of whimsical, neatly stacked stones here and there. These subtle yet inescapably manmade signatures on the natural landscape are wonderfully simple examples of how working with stone satisfies many impulses: the need to create and work with our hands, to recognize or impose order in nature, and to appreciate natural beauty. The ancient Chinese used stone extensively in their gardens, not only for practical terraces and walls, but as landscaping features with symbolic resonance; they called stone the "bones of heaven and earth."

Whether used "as found" or quarried and cut to shape, stone "bones"—weighty, practical, durable, and beautiful—are natural building blocks that practically beg to be featured in your landscape. Use them to create garden benches, either as the focus of attention or as a subtle accent. Build a stone-lined fire pit, or stand tall stones on end to mark an entryway or a hidden garden feature. Even a few fascinating boulders can be grouped together to fashion a bold or unusual stone sculpture and add just the right finishing touch to your landscape.

◄ A "COUNCIL RING" CREATES AN OPEN INVITATION for campfires and family gatherings at this tiny northern Wisconsin cabin. Built with fieldstones collected from family homesteads in both Wisconsin and Norway, the rustic stonework creates an outdoor living area that doesn't compete with the natural scenery.

Benches

No GARDEN IS COMPLETE without a place to sit, relax, and enjoy the view. While seating can be built out of a variety of materials, none have the visual weight of stone, and nothing compares with stone for natural beauty, durability, and low maintenance. In a small garden, a simple block of stone or small boulder at just the right height creates a charming accent and a welcoming seat. Larger two- or three-person stone benches—whether rustic or intricately carved—can create a focal point in bigger gardens. But remember that stone benches aren't made for lingering; stone can be hard and cold, making it uncomfortable to sit on for long periods. Use stone benches where visits are brief, and place them where they'll get morning sun and afternoon shade. Here they'll feel invitingly warm and dry early in the day and refreshingly cool later on when the temperature rises.

▲ DISCRETELY TUCKED INTO THE STONE retaining wall, this slab bench doesn't intrude on the landscape yet offers convenient overflow seating when needed. Located in full sun rather than shaded by plantings, it will feel warm and dry most of the day.

► A SIMPLE BENCH made of limestone blocks offers a quiet waypoint for listening to water coursing over the stones and contemplating the surroundings, provides a pleasing contrast to the stones and gravel along the streambed, and complements the Japanese-inspired design of this Missouri moss garden.

◄ WHILE THE BACK OF A BENCH that's built into a retaining wall can be dry-stacked like the wall around it, a large flat stone creates a more comfortable backrest and visually emphasizes that this spot is meant for sitting.

▼ A LONG CUT STONE SLAB set into a rubble stone wall offers unobtrusive seating and helps define this garden's border. Benches that are protected from behind—either by a wall or by plantings—feel more sheltered and comforting than those placed out in the open.

▲ ONCE LOCATED IN A SMALLER, more formal garden, the 4-ft.-long granite slab and two supporting cast-concrete bases that make up this bench were moved here to provide a quiet resting place along this woodland path, which borders a dry creek bed.

Designing a Stone Bench

WHETHER YOU BUILD A freestanding stone bench or incorporate one into a retaining wall, look for large, flat-surfaced slabs of stone between 3 ft. and 5 ft. in length; more comfortable to sit on, these are also more manageable (though still heavy) than irregular stone. For easeful seating, the top of your bench should be between 16 in. and 18 in. off the ground, with a 21-in. seat depth. Securely support the slab with substantial stones buried at least 6 in. into the ground. Stone or gravel underneath the bench will drain more quickly after rain than a grass or dirt base.

► GARDEN SEATING OUGHT to offer a clean, dry place for the feet. Though this simple stone bench is actually sited in the planting bed, the path's stone and gravel surface extends under the bench, keeping feet out of the mulch.

▲ A GARDEN BENCH SHOULD BE located in a part of the landscape that invites frequent—though not necessarily lengthy—visits and that offers a compelling vista. Backed up to plantings, this bench also feels comfortably sheltered rather than exposed from behind.

◄ THE STILLNESS OF A POND invites contemplation and reflection, making it an ideal setting for a stone bench.

Landscaping Features

Simple stone cairns built by the Druids thousands of years ago to mark holy places and burial sites can still be found in the British Isles. In Japan and China, traditional gardens are renowned for their use of stone, not only for walls, terraces, and steps, but also in ornamental, symbolic, and spiritual roles. From the famed Egyptian pyramids at Giza to the carved volcanic moai of the Easter Islands, the human impulse to arrange stones for both functional and symbolic purposes is strong and cuts across all cultures. There are many traditions that you can draw on as you seek out and arrange special stones, creating compositions that serve both artistic and practical purposes and leaving your own signature on the landscape.

▲ **BUILT WITH GRANITE BLOCKS** of varying color and size, this fire pit is intended to be practical, but its geometry and texture also bring a sculptural and meditative quality to the landscape, even during the daytime.

▶ **PERCHED ATOP A** loosely constructed stone pyramid, this small ceramic lantern helps guide the way toward a nearby stone labyrinth. Filled with citronella oil, the lamp helps keep mosquitoes away when lit, while the combination of stone and fire brings a meditative focus to this woodland setting.

▲ BUILT WITH LOCAL RIVER ROCK mortared around a brick-lined firebox and clay-tile chimney flue, this beehive fireplace is perfect for toasting "s'mores" at family cookouts. The dry-laid tumbled concrete block retaining wall and stamped concrete patio contrast with the free-form quality of the fireplace.

◄ WITH ITS BOWL-SHAPED HOLLOW, this well-placed stone collects rainwater and serves as both reflecting pool and ground-level bird-bath. The stone's rich rust hue adds an attractive year-round accent to the garden.

BOULDERS, BEDROCK, AND STANDING STONES

▲ DIAGONAL BANDS OF WHITE quartz run through these matching granite posts, which mark the entrance to an herb garden. Set on a stone column and shaped like an open globe, the equatorial sundial is the garden's centerpiece.

▲ THOUGH IT LOOKS LIKE STONE, this faux basalt water basin is hollow-molded using a lightweight mixture of concrete and fiberglass. At about 60 lbs., compared to 600 lbs. or more for the real thing, it looks genuine and is easily handled by one or two people.

▲ SALVAGED CUT GRANITE FOUNDATION stones frame a small cave and create a focal point that relieves the mass of this Maine fieldstone retaining wall. A small, still pool inside the cave rewards further investigation and provides the shallow cave with the illusion of depth.

▲ FOUND IN A LOCAL OKLAHOMA STONEYARD, these standing stones mark the entryway into this small and informal Asian-influenced garden. When winter comes, the stones and the horizontal stonework surrounding the koi pond maintain drama and visual interest in the snow-covered landscape.

▲ A RICHLY SYMBOLIC PART of Celtic religious tradition, labyrinths represent the physical and spiritual journey toward the sacred center, or *omphalos*, where heaven and earth are joined. This contemporary interpretation was woven among the site's trees and was built with local Vermont river rock.

Planting a Stone

To keep a tall stone from tipping over, it must be set into the ground properly. Begin by digging a hole that is about one-third the length of the stone and about three times the width of the post. While this kind of deep, narrow hole can be dug with a shovel, it's easier to use a post-hole digger (available at most hardware stores and home centers for rent or purchase). Next, place a 3-in.- or 4-in.-thick flat stone in the bottom of the hole; if none are available, you can mix up a 40-lb. bag of concrete mix and place that in the hole, letting it cure before setting the post.

Place your stone in the hole gently so that it doesn't crack the base. Plumb the stone so that it's vertical, then adjust it for appearance; once you're satisfied, backfill the bottom 6 in. or so with crushed stones or coarse gravel, tamping the stone firmly with the head of a sledgehammer. Continue adding backfill and tamping every 6 in. until the hole is filled to about 4 in. below grade, add a layer of black plastic or weed barrier over the backfill, and then cover with topsoil.

▶ SETTING A STONE POST To adequately support a 6-ft.-high stone that is 6 in. wide, dig a hole that is 2 ft. deep and 18 in. wide. Adjust the stone so that it is plumb and looks balanced.

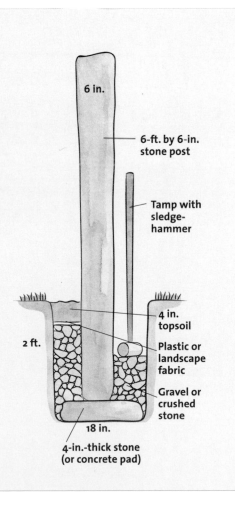

6 in.

6-ft. by 6-in. stone post

Tamp with sledge-hammer

4 in. topsoil

2 ft.

Plastic or landscape fabric

Gravel or crushed stone

18 in.

4-in.-thick stone (or concrete pad)

PRACTICAL STONEWORK

▲ SIMPLER TO BUILD THAN A FIREPLACE, a stone fire pit recalls childhood campfire memories and makes a perfect weekend project. Sparks fall harmlessly on the large flat stones surrounding the fire pit, which also create a minipatio for the feet of campers seated nearby.

▲ SUPPORTED BY ELABORATELY CARVED stone pilasters, this stone lintel was originally used in an interior fireplace but was later recycled for use in this retaining wall. The weathered firewood niche creates a ruinlike accent against the wall's tightly fitted stones.

▶ A MAN-MADE STREAM trickles down this moss-covered Missouri hillside and under a gracefully arched stone bridge, made with a reclaimed section of granite street curb left over from a St. Louis public works project. Crushed gravel lines the gullies and helps keep them from eroding.

▲ THOUGH BUILT TO THE SAME STANDARDS as an interior fireplace, the large size and irregular shapes of the native fieldstone used in its construction give this outdoor fireplace an almost primitive look that matches the relaxed atmosphere of this Vermont vacation home.

▶ THIS BEAUTIFUL AND FUNCTIONAL stone design offers gardeners and visitors access to a peaceful spot. A variation on the octagram, or eight-pointed star, this symbol is often used to represent the cycle of time and the power of regeneration and return in pagan and Wiccan traditions.

▼ STONE CAN BE INCORPORATED with other natural materials to create compelling yet practical furniture. This Tennessee sandstone tabletop is supported by locust trunks held together by a threaded rod and a ¼-in.-thick steel sheet screwed into the branch ends and supporting the stone slab.

▲ MEASURING ONLY 8 FT. TALL, this dry stacked pool house was built around the wooden walls of a former well house. With a roof of hand-split cedar shakes, the tiny structure complements the architecture of the nearby English cottage-style Martha's Vineyard home.

◄ BECAUSE OF ITS RELATIVELY SMALL size and circular shape, this mortared stone amphitheater has a sculptural quality that invites closer inspection. Because its purpose is ambiguous, it adds an element of mystery and discovery to the landscape.

Sculpture

Whether large in scale and prominently featured or a diminutive objet d'art awaiting serendipitous discovery, a stone sculpture adds an intriguing element to any garden. Carved stone statues are a legacy of the Greeks; Europeans imported the tradition to their formal gardens during the Romantic period; and lifelike carvings of people, animals, and urns are often found in today's formal gardens. More likely, though, your landscape design will reflect more modern and naturalistic sensibilities, and the sculptural forms you choose will reflect your own culture, interests, and experiences. For example, a personal artifact, like a carved stone from an exotic trip, makes a wonderful garden accent. Remember that even though your sculpture may be made of stone, its placement isn't set in stone: It may take several tries before you find its ideal location. But that's part of the fun.

▲ PLACED NEAR WATER OR AT INTERSECTIONS, stone lanterns were used in traditional Japanese gardens to light pathways at night and to symbolize themes of passage (above). Most often carved from granite, but also from sandstone or even lava rock, some are predrilled and can be fitted with electric lamps, making them functional as well as ornamental. In cold or wet climates, a *yukimi-gama* (or snow-viewing lantern) is designed with an overhanging roof to shed rain and capture snow, which dramatizes and accentuates the lantern's form in the landscape (top).

▲ A SMALL ORNAMENTAL DETAIL, such as this carved sculpture nestled in a river-rock border, can add an element of surprise and interest to a landscape. Here the stonework and plantings reflect the subtropical theme of this Portland, Oregon, courtyard garden.

▲ SUNDIALS CAN BE USED to create interesting focal points in a variety of contemporary garden designs. Horizontal sundials consist of a dial plate marked in hour lines (the sun moves westward 15 degrees per hour) and a vertical gnomon, which casts a shadow. A sundial can be set low on a rock (above) or at eye level on a stone pedestal (top), but to be accurate it should be located in a sunny, level spot and oriented with the gnomon parallel to the earth's axis.

◄ RISING OUT OF THE EULALIA GRASS, this sculpture's vaguely anthropomorphic shape offers an intriguing hint of the surprises awaiting discovery in the garden beyond. Composed of stone, found objects, and pieces of reused concrete, the tall sculpture marks the intersection of this California garden's two main axes.

5

Pools, Ponds, and Fountains

Transparent and formless, water is the natural antithesis of stone. Yet when water and stone are combined, as they often are in nature, water gives mute stone a voice that can range from the delicate whisper of a quiet pool to the rushing sound of a babbling brook; stone gives water shape and form—a pebble beach, a dramatic waterfall. Re-creating this natural relationship in your landscape with a swimming pool or decorative pond, a stream or waterfall, or a simple water basin or elaborate fountain will invigorate your landscape, breathing life into it and infusing it with energy. Whether it is used as an accent or as a primary construction material, stone will perfectly complement any water feature. For example, stone is well-suited for paving around a pool, of course, but with the addition of a few well-placed boulders, a stone wall, or even a rocky waterfall splashing gently into it, a pool can often blend better into the landscape. Pond liners and water pumps make it possible to create beautiful—and affordable—streams, ponds, and waterfalls in your garden; stone will help you bring the magic of water to life.

◄ RECIRCULATED WATER FLOWING OVER moss-covered stone ledges and past native plantings creates a mesmerizing sound that can be heard from the nearby master bedroom of a home in Maine. The thoughtful and well-engineered design gives this 60-ft. man-made stream a natural look.

Pools

O FTEN RIGIDLY GEOMETRIC IN SHAPE, a large, formal swimming pool can dominate a landscape. Of course, stone adapts easily to an orderly landscape design; for instance, cut stone pavers with a honed finish are a logical choice around a pool because they offer good traction even when wet, and cut stone coping to frame the pool's edge is a nice upgrade from concrete. But while stone beautifully and practically enhances the design of a formal pool, it is also a logical choice for pools that blend in rather than stand out from the landscape. Whether your pool is custom-built or a manufactured model, you can incorporate stone, using a variety of strategies, to soften its look. For example, use irregular flagstones instead of rectilinear cut pavers for the pool deck, or incorporate stone walls, boulders, or even a natural-looking waterfall into the pool's overall design.

▲ THE "VANISHING EDGE" OF THIS MAINE POOL drops over a smooth coping of a locally quarried green slate known as Monson slate and into a surrounding "moat," which frames the pool and collects the water for recirculating. Veneered with Corinthian granite to match the extensive retaining walls used elsewhere on this sloped site, the exterior face of the pool echoes the rugged Casco Bay coastline. And the pool deck's Pennsylvania bluestone pavers demonstrate the wide color variations inherent in this popular sandstone.

◄ ▼ THOUGH THE MAIN DECK surrounding this pool (left) is concrete (stamped to give it a stonelike appearance), the circular spa (below) is surrounded by flagstones, offering a more casual, rustic ambience for this intimate setting. Water coursing down a boulder-strewn "stream" and falling into the pool gives the landscape a natural look while adding the soothing sound of a waterfall (bottom).

► THOUGH THE SETTING AND SHAPE are formal, the delicate weaving of lawn and flagstones that surrounds this southern California pool softens the composition and gives it an archaic—though perfectly preserved—quality suggesting a more ancient civilization.

◄ ▼ DESIGNED TO COMPLEMENT THE ARCHITECTURE and the view, this small New Mexico "spool" (or combination spa and pool) was built using a variety of types of local stone to help it blend into the desert landscape. It has a sloped, beach-style flagstone entrance instead of a conventional set of steps (left).

Using Stone to Landscape a Swimming Pool

EVEN A SMALL SWIMMING pool occupies a considerable amount of actual—and perceived—real estate. By integrating stone into the design, you can help the pool look like a settled rather than an artificial part of the landscape. For example, when underlying bedrock encountered during construction created a taller-than-expected finish grade for this Massachusetts pool, landscape architect Jim Donahue designed terraced stone retaining walls to ease the nearly 8-ft. transition between yard and pool levels (top right). The stone staircase that steps up the retaining walls and onto the exposed aggregate concrete deck opens directly into a view across the pool of a natural-looking stone waterfall (below). Boulders and plantings on the hillside behind the pool continue the woodsy look begun by the large rocks that flank the waterfall along the pool's edge. Instead of a diving board, there is a large diving rock that cantilevers out over the water's surface (bottom right). Finally, a flagstone path leads under and away from the white arched arbor (built to screen the pool's heating and filtration system) and past the small garden shed built to provide storage and to screen nearby road noise and views.

▲ INTERRUPTED BY A PLANTING BED, the fieldstone retaining walls that step up nearly 8 ft. from lawn to pool create a gradual and natural-looking transition between the two levels. The wide stone steps offer an open invitation to enter the pool area.

▶ AN ARCHED ARBOR INTENTIONALLY PLACED directly across the pool focuses attention on the natural landscape and makes the pool feel like a part of a larger composition. Boulders flanking the pool's edge continue the woodland theme introduced by the waterfall and adjacent hillside.

◀ THOUGH THE PRIMARY DECKING SURFACE bordering the pool is exposed-aggregate concrete, boulders, plantings, and a small waterfall on the far "shore" of the pool directly opposite the built-in spa help blend it into its woodland surroundings.

Ponds

With a small pond, you can transform an ordinary backyard into a sanctuary. Plants will flourish there, wildlife will be attracted to it, and the pond's still waters will create a mood of serenity that will refresh your spirit and delight your senses. Unlike larger swimming pools, a pond doesn't have to dominate your landscape or overwhelm your budget. There are a number of widely available materials, including circulating pumps, prefabricated rigid fiberglass forms, and flexible rubber and vinyl pond liners, that make pond construction relatively easy and inexpensive, and a pond can be scaled to suit any size space. Stone will transform your man-made pond into a magical spot; placed around the edges of your pond, it will conceal and protect the liner; arranged in creative or natural-looking designs, it can make you forget that you're still in your own backyard.

◀▲ THIS SMALL POND IS PART of a terrace; large, smooth, light-colored Shenandoah flagstones ease the transition between walking surface and pond edge, while contrasting darker Sonoma fieldstone boulders mark the edges of the pond. The far side of the pond is supported by a mortared retaining wall composed of Kennesaw stone and pieces of broken recycled concrete (left). Planting pockets and tucked mortar joints help blend the wall and pond together (above).

▲ A SMALL STREAM THAT STEPS DOWN nearly 16 ft. of elevation on this sloped site connects a series of five small stone- and boulder-lined ponds, including a gunite spa. A filtration system keeps the water clean as it travels from bottom to top.

◄ CONNECTICUT BLUESTONE FLAGSTONES step around to one side of this pond to create a relaxed gathering area that features a stone fire ring. The jumble of boulders lining the pond's perimeter creates a natural setting for the small stream splashing into it.

Planning a Pond

With flexible rubber or vinyl pool liners, ponds can be built in all shapes and sizes. A basically oval design without a fussy shoreline is the easiest to build and minimizes dead areas where water can't flow freely through the pond's filtration system. If you plan to stock your pond with fish or sun-loving plants, site it to ensure it receives 5 to 8 hours of sunlight a day (top right). To prevent overheating flora or fauna, make ponds large enough (over 50 sq. ft.) and deep enough (more than 30 in.) so the water temperature doesn't fluctuate excessively and fish can winter over.

You can create "shelves" that will support stones, plants, and the rocks that will line the pool's edge (both hiding the liner and holding it in place) by excavating your pond so that it has multiple levels. The stone shelf should be approximately the same width as the stones you'll be using and about 8 in. below water level. The plant shelf, where potted aquatics can be placed, should be about 12 in. to 18 in. below water level. The deepest part of the pond is where the filtration system will be situated (bottom right).

▲ LARGER STONES THAT EDGE A POND conceal and protect the pond liner, while smaller cobbles and gravel beneath the water's surface make a good pond "floor." Potted aquatics, such as these water iris, thrive in open sunlit spaces.

▶ POND SHELVES SUPPORT THE stones that line the shoreline and hold the liner in place. Sloping shelf walls slightly allows ice to slide up when the pond freezes rather than push against—and possibly pierce—the pond liner.

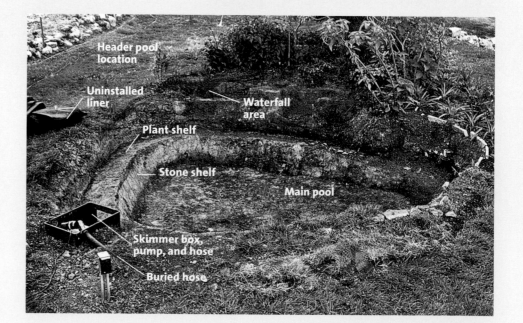

Header pool location

Uninstalled liner

Waterfall area

Plant shelf

Stone shelf

Main pool

Skimmer box, pump, and hose

Buried hose

◀▲ SITED AT THE BASE OF A HILLSIDE terraced with gardens and laced with paths, this small fishpond offers a quiet focal point for the eye and a calm and sunny resting spot. The stone retaining wall along the back of the pond (left) emphasizes the soothing horizontal sightlines created by the water while helping to anchor the pond to the hillside.

▼ A SMALL STREAM SPLASHES into this quiet koi pond, which is lined with a mixture of smooth California waterwash boulders and darker, lichen-covered Buzzard Canyon moss rock, a natural choice for a pond in a shady setting.

Pond Safety

BEFORE YOU BEGIN EXCAVATING your pond, consult your local building department to find out about any necessary permits and enclosure requirements. Building codes often require that ponds over 3 ft. deep be protected by a fence, but any body of water can be a hazard to children. If there are youngsters in your household, think about postponing pond construction until they are older, and consider how accessible your yard is to neighbors' young ones as well. Also, because electricity and water can be a fatal combination, make sure all pump and lighting wiring meets electrical code requirements.

▲ **THE CENTERPIECE OF A VERMONT GARDEN** that's nestled slightly below grade, this small semicircular formal pond gets plenty of sunlight and provides a good habitat for fish and plantings. The smooth bluestone topping the pool's low retaining wall provides an ideal spot for sitting.

▼ **CONNECTED TO THE VERMONT "MAINLAND"** by a footbridge, this small island is sheltered beneath the graceful branches of a weeping willow, a tree that thrives in moist soil (bottom). A miniature waterfall built with river rock splashes gently into the pond, which is home to a school of goldfish (below).

Plants for Pools and Ponds

THE KINDS OF PLANTS THAT WILL THRIVE in or around your water garden will depend on your region's climate, how sunny or shady your pond is, and the size and depth of your pond. To contrast the horizontal character of water and stone, choose plants that grow tall, such as irises, ferns, and ornamental grasses. When selecting plants for your pond, keep things simple: A few plants set in groupings of at least three will look more natural and less busy than a hodgepodge of plants sprinkled around the pond.

Plants that thrive in moist conditions fall into three basic categories: shallow-water plants that grow in wet soil around the edges of a pond, such as marsh marigold and varieties of water iris (right); plants that need total submersion, such as water lotus and water lilies and some varieties of water iris (below); and floaters, such as water clover and water lettuce, which drift around the surface of the pond, dragging their roots behind them. Some hardy perennials can be left in the pool year-round, while tropicals (such as water lotus) will either need to be replanted every year or brought indoors in cold weather.

▲ A COLORFUL STAND OF BLUE FLAG IRIS emerges from the water-covered rocks that edge this water garden. While some iris varieties grow well in soggy soil, some prefer deeper water and should be grown in pots placed between 4 in. and 12 in. below the water's surface.

◄ PONDS CAN support a variety of different types of water-loving plants, including low-profile water lilies which bloom over and over again all summer long. Ornamental grasses and irises add a vertical dimension to the composition and help integrate the pond with the surrounding garden.

Streams and Waterfalls

WHILE THE STILL WATERS OF A POOL OR POND bring a calming influence to a landscape, streams and waterfalls infuse it with energy. Whether moving slowly or rushing in a cascade, water flowing past, over, and around rock creates dynamic tension. Where pools and ponds bring focus to a landscape and create a kind of static composition, a stream runs through the landscape like a story, connecting one part with another in a narrative filled with sound and splashes of shadow and light. Of course, the tale told by your stream depends on its style. You can create a stream that imitates nature or build a highly stylized watercourse that interprets and tames nature to suit the landscape's character. Waterfalls, too, can be either imitative or stylized; either way, stone is the ideal building material with which to put a body of water into motion and bring it to life.

▲ A SERIES OF NEARLY A DOZEN small outlets buried in various locations along this "weeping wall" allow water to seep out and flow down the wall's face, into the rivulet, and toward a collecting pool that contains a recirculating pump.

▶ WATERFALLS VARY IN SIZE and shape, and the sounds they make range from a whisper to a roar, but their dramatic impact on a landscape is a universal constant. This slender column of water sings as it splashes over rock and into the pool below.

▲ RENOVATIONS EXPANDED THE FOOTPRINT of this old Maine home, requiring a culvert to direct seasonal runoff underneath the addition and into this drainage channel. Plantings and local fieldstone give the channel the quality of a natural stream, and granite slabs make it easy to cross.

◀ A COMBINATION OF SMALL natural moss rocks and larger, hand-colored artificial rocks (made with wire forms and spray-on, fiberglass-reinforced concrete) were used to create a series of cascading pools along this naturally occurring—but dry—ravine, which is spanned by a 60-ft. wooden foot bridge.

NATURAL-LOOKING STREAMS

▲ CASCADING BETWEEN TWO SMALL PONDS, this series of miniature waterfalls brings a garden to life with its sound and gentle fury. Flat rocks in the stream help spread the water into sheets, magnifying the visual impact of this self-contained water-course's relatively small volume of water.

◄▲ THOUGH MEASURING ONLY a few inches wide, this slender stream expands the compact backyard of this California home by filling it with the sound of running water as it flows from one small pond to the other. Large boulders (top) effectively mark transitions in streams and are useful where water changes directions or to create a quiet eddy.

A River Doesn't Usually Run Through It

SUBURBAN BACKYARDS ARE OFTEN SMALL, rectangular, and flat, presenting a topography that challenges the design skills of those who are looking to inject vitality into their landscape. While a water structure is a great way to spruce up a blah backyard, you might want to consider landscape architect Konrad Gauder's creative solution for this Washington state home: a dry streambed.

Essentially a water structure without the water, this rock-lined "streambed" bisects the backyard diagonally, helping to create a sense of depth on the small lot. Rounded river cobbles line the bottom of the creek, while larger locally quarried basalt boulders placed along the edges help define the streambed and give it a more realistic look. A series of berms (low earth walls) were built to surround the streambed, creating a rolling rather than flat terrain and helping with the illusion that water courses through the backyard. Because the streambed was intentionally built so that it follows a downward grade and leads to a concealed storm drain, stormwater runoff actually does run through it during rainstorms. When the weather is sunny, a bubbling boulder fountain at the stream's "source" enhances the illusion of running water.

◀▲ CROSSED BY A FLAGSTONE PATH, the dry "streambed" that meanders across the back of this suburban backyard looks realistic and also functions to direct stormwater runoff toward a storm drain. Rounded river cobbles from a highway construction site line the bottom, while larger basalt boulders and plantings help define the edge and reflect the contours of the berms flanking the stream.

▲ **A SLAB STONE BRIDGE** crosses over a small stream connecting two ponds in this extensive Vermont garden. Built with a mix of both rounded river stones and flatter stones that create small waterfalls and pools along the stream's course, the design perfectly parallels nature.

Designing for Drainage

WHEN LARGE HOMES ARE BUILT on small lots in densely populated urban or suburban areas, stormwater drainage becomes an issue. Conventional solutions—such as concrete flumes—for handling runoff and directing it away from homes and into street drains are generally effective, though not particularly aesthetically pleasing to avid gardeners. In a creative solution to this common problem, landscape designer Paula Refi designed a streamlike swale, or depression, that channels stormwater from the back of this Atlanta home, along the side of the house, and out to a storm sewer in the street (top right).

To slow the velocity of the runoff, the stream meanders gently as it slopes away from the collecting swale at the back of the house and runs down toward the street. Substantial river slicks of varying sizes line the streambed, also helping to slow the water while preventing erosion and providing a framework for the plantings that line the stream (bottom right). As the streambed passes the side of the house, a flow-through fence intersects it, providing security and a sense of privacy between front yard and back; here, flat stepping stones placed in the streambed turn the stream into a footpath (below).

▲▼ THIS DRY STREAMBED handles significant stormwater runoff (upward of a foot or more in a typical rain), directing it into a storm sewer located at street level (above). A wide range of plantings, including boldly colorful ornamentals in the sunny front yard and deeply rooted, moisture-loving species in the shady and wetter backyard, help secure the banks of the 150-ft.-long stream. Grouped to emulate the look of a natural creek, the stones control erosion while also creating planting pockets that enhance this Atlanta home's landscape.

▲ SMALL TREES THAT ADAPT WELL to occasional flooding, like river birch and dwarf Southern magnolia, ferns, and a few shrubs line the streambed as it passes through the narrow side yard. Large, flat stepping stones placed among the river slicks provide secure, dry footing in any weather.

Designing a Stream

Like ponds, streams are built with waterproof rubber or PVC liners; stones conceal and protect the liner while giving the stream a natural look, and a small pump supplies and recirculates water. Here are some design tips to help your man-made stream mimic nature.

- Choose stones that look like they belong in your landscape. Bare stones look best in sunny spots, while mossy stones are found in shady settings.
- Scale stones to the landscape. Large stones will overpower a small, intimate stream, while small stones will be overwhelmed in a larger setting. A combination of small, medium, and large stones best reflects a natural stream design.
- Follow your landscape's natural drainage patterns, and make sure your stream has adequate slope (falling about 1 in. for every 8 ft. of length).
- Lay stones and rocks down rather than standing them upright; this is how they're found in nature.
- Choose and arrange stone to reflect the stream's style. A meandering meadow stream is broad with even banks and usually features smooth, eroded stone and rounded cobbles. A rushing mountain stream more often flows over sharp-edged boulders, is narrow and shallow, and has uneven banks.

▲ NATIVE GRANITE STEPPING STONES, each about 30 in. in diameter, provide an avenue of travel up the middle of the stream in this Japanese-style garden. The shallow streambed is made with reinforced concrete lined with thin granite slabs and washed river rock mortared in place.

▶ THOUGH THE SETTING is suburban southern California, the angular, multi-hued rocks used to build this water structure suggest a rushing mountain stream.

▲ FLOWING OUT OF A SMALL artificial pond, this babbling brook brings the sights and sounds of streaming water to this otherwise waterless Vermont landscape. While part of the design is deliberate, some stones were randomly placed, making their distribution look more natural.

FORMAL CHANNELS AND RILLS

▶ **WATER SPILLS OVER THE EDGES** of this small marble fountain and falls into a stone-edged and pebble-lined rill (a tiny brook, also called a runnel), which circulates it through the surrounding California citrus garden. Traditional hand-cut and painted Moroccan tiles line the bottom of the fountain, while the spout is carved from alabaster.

▼ **A MEDITERRANEAN TRADITION**—a courtyard featuring a formal geometric pool connected to a fountain by a rill—is given a New England twist with the extensive use of granite and fieldstone. Though built of concrete, the rill and pool are lined with old grey granite slabs.

▲ A TIDY WATERCOURSE bisects the stone steps leading up to this California home's trellis-covered terrace, adding the sights and sounds of running water to the formally composed, garden-lined landscape.

◄ ORIGINATING OUT OF A SMALL, spouting fountain on an upper terrace, water cascades down a few steps before running through a straight and narrow rill and spilling into a larger pool in the garden below.

WATERFALLS

▲ WATER SPILLING FROM THE LEAD-COATED copper gutter topping a sandblasted concrete retaining wall falls nearly 6 ft. before splashing into a rock-lined pool. The chain leader dropping down from the roof gutter reflects the strong Japanese influence in this home's landscape design.

▲ A GROUP OF SMALL POOLS stacked one atop another are connected by a series of streams and waterfalls. With a flip of a switch, the water flow turns on or off, changing the character of the pools from loud and lively to quiet and contemplative.

◄ WITH A VERTICAL DROP of nearly 15 ft. and a flow rate of 150 gallons per minute, this two-level waterfall generates plenty of visual and auditory impact. The water feature is contained within a reinforced concrete structure, and the granite stones are set onto concrete footings.

Designing a Waterfall

IN MANY RESPECTS, an artificial waterfall is simply an artificial stream turned on its end. Both require a waterproof liner, a pump, plumbing, and electricity. Yet there are many ways to add distinguishing details to your waterfall. Here are some tips:

- The key to a waterfall's character lies in its lip, or the edge over which the water spills. To create a broad sheet of water, use a wide flat stone. For a denser column of water, channel the stream between two rocks.
- Pushing the lip stone out from the waterfall's base will create a vertical curtain or column of water. Moving the same stone back from the face of the waterfall will cause the water to gurgle and splash as it nears its descent.
- The sound that your waterfall makes on impact depends on whether the water drops into a pool or onto rocks. After the waterfall is built, you can move rocks around to create the most pleasing combination of sound and water patterns. The farther the water falls, the more dramatic and intense will be the sight and sound.

About Stream and Pond Liners

THE STRONGEST STREAM AND POND liners are made of synthetic rubber. Butyl rubber liners are black and range in thickness from 30 mil to 45 mil (or thousands of an inch). EPDM (ethylene propylene diene monomer polymer) rubber liners are gray and usually are sold in 45-mil thickness only. Cheaper PVC (polyvinyl chloride) plastic liners aren't as strong or stretchy as rubber, so they are more likely to split or crack. Thicker liners are stronger and more puncture resistant, while thinner liners are more flexible and easier to work with around complex shapes. Using premade liners (versus custom) will help cut costs.

▲ EVEN A SMALL VOLUME OF WATER speaks in a loud voice when the distance that the water falls is significant. This water falls on a flat rock before flowing into the pool below, emphasizing the effect.

▲ THOUGH OCCUPYING ONLY A FEW square feet of real estate, this cisternlike pool's impact on the landscape is amplified by the water falling into it, which is clearly audible both from the surrounding garden and the nearby house.

▲ IN A DESIGN THAT COMBINES RUSTIC, irregularly shaped flagstones with a formal sensibility, water cascades down the shallow steps connecting this circular spa with a lower-level pool, suggesting a natural waterfall.

▲ FISH FLOURISH IN THE MAN-MADE, cement-and-gunite-lined pond that lies at the base of this natural-looking Connecticut waterfall. Pumped by a 1-horsepower sewage pump with adjustable valves that control the volume, water flows over both the main falls and through the two fissures on either side.

Water Basins and Fountains

▲ **CARVED FROM BLACK GRANITE**, this stone water basin presents a sculptural focal point at the edge of this flagstone terrace. Small, smooth river stones that surround the water basin suggest the presence of more water while marking the transition between the terrace and the surrounding landscape.

URING THE RENAISSANCE, CARVED STONE fountains became a dominant feature in European gardens, and certainly this tradition still has resonance in a formal landscape design. More likely, however, your gardens will be more casual, and a large, ornately carved fountain might look out of place. Still, this compact method of introducing the sights and sounds of moving water into a garden can be accomplished with more informal fountain designs. Many garden and home centers offer preassembled stone fountains in a range of styles—all you need to do is provide power—but it's also relatively easy to create your own fountain design that can be as splashy or as subtle as you'd like. If you'd prefer not to invest in a small recirculating pump and some plastic tubing, you can set up a simple water basin that will quietly and gracefully collect and hold rainwater for your contemplation.

▶ **CALLED A "SOLSTICE FOUNTAIN"** by its builder, this south-facing fountain features sunburst mosaics composed of smooth, multicolored stones set into mortar. Water is piped to the center of each sunburst through ¼-in. flexible copper tubing, then drops into a small pool below.

▲ SALVAGED FROM CHINA'S YANGTZE RIVER VALLEY, this small antique limestone mill wheel makes an ideal water fountain in this lily pond. Mill wheels can vary in size up to 7 ft. in diameter and can also be used for garden sculpture or patio tables.

▲ WATER SPILLS FROM A CAST-CONCRETE BASIN into a circle of small washed river stone contained by a cast iron ring. The irregularly shaped fieldstones that surround the ring of pebbles contrast with the smooth geometric forms of the water basin and catchment.

▲ PART OF A PRACTICAL AND SCULPTURAL rainwater drainage system, a stone-filled concrete box collects water running down chain leaders and diverts the overflow into a storm drain. An alternative to downspouts, chain leaders minimize splashing while suggesting the flow of water even in dry weather.

▲ NESTLED INTO THE INTERSECTION of two low stone walls that define the back edge of a Portland, Oregon, courtyard garden, this 6-ft. by 10-ft. fishpond features a simple fountain that helps aerate and circulate the water while providing a gentle sound of splashing water.

◀ PERCHED ON A FIELDSTONE "ISLAND" surrounded by ornamental grasses and smooth, black Mexican river stone, this copper water basin is the focal point of a viewing garden.

A Simple Garden Fountain

IF YOU CAN'T SEEM TO FIND **the right fountain for your garden, consider making your own.** Besides a few hours of work, all that it requires is a small piece of pond liner, a large plastic bucket or barrel to act as the reservoir, a small pump, some plumbing and a few connectors, and an attractive vessel. Most of this goes underground, making the installation rather permanent, so choose a well-loved location and one that has a GFCI-protected outlet nearby (extension cords are NOT a safe substitute). You may need an electrician.

You'll need to dig a hole for the fountain's reservoir, which houses the recirculating pump and holds the water supply. The pond liner drapes over the buried bucket and directs water that splashes out of the fountain back into the reservoir. You'll also need to place some sort of porous support (like a round barbecue grill) over the reservoir to support the fountain vessel as well as the rocks that you use to embellish it. While this design shows a ceramic urn (right), the plastic pipe that emerges from out of the reservoir can be routed through other sculptural garden pieces or an attractive rock arrangement (top right).

Grill **PVC pipe**

Plastic liner **Plastic tubing**

Reservoir **Pump**

▲ A SIMPLE GARDEN FOUNTAIN Water contained in the reservoir is pumped up through a plastic pipe, where it bubbles out of the urn and splashes over its sides before draining back through the grid-supported rock and into the reservoir.

▲ SMOOTH, WATER-WORN ROCKS supported by a concealed metal grid create a naturalistic setting for this small garden fountain. Underneath the grid, the water collects into a large bucket and is pumped back to the surface by a small recirculating pump.

▲ WITH AN AMPHORA-LIKE SHAPE that hints at the classical origins of formal gardens, this large decorative ceramic urn makes an ideal water fountain. Placed atop a hidden reservoir and surrounded by stones and plantings, the fountain brings a small splash of delight to this corner of the garden.

6

Finishing Touches

There are dozens of ways that stone can be used to enhance the appearance of your home and gardens. For example, you may want to focus on your front entrance, a central focal point that directly impacts your home's overall curb appeal and creates such an important first impression on visitors. To improve the way it looks and functions, use stone to pave pathways and steps that lead up to it, and build stone walls to help define the space. At the same time, don't neglect the other entries into your house; here, stone can be used to extend your home's living areas into the backyard, connecting indoor and outdoor spaces in both practical and decorative ways. Dress up your driveway with a stone wall to help separate it from adjacent lawn or garden areas, or add stone borders or curbing. Or simply use either cut or natural stone to edge a path or a garden, giving your landscape definition while keeping planting and pathway materials in their place. All around the house, stone can add just the right finishing touch to your landscape design.

◄ PART OF AN EXTENSIVE MAKEOVER of this suburban Georgia home that also involved replacing a traditional front lawn with a naturalistic woodland garden, granite cobblestones were used to widen the driveway. The cobblestones also reflect the granite walls framing the steps leading up to the entryway.

Entryways

Your front entry is your home's public face; here is where visitors catch their first glimpse of your family's character. While front entries beckon guests in, rear and side entries extend your home's living spaces out into the landscape, inviting family and friends to step back out again. Well-designed entryways ease the transition between interior and exterior spaces, helping to create a safe, comfortable, and hospitable mood while unifying architecture and landscape so that your home feels well-connected with its surrounding environment. Stone can play a key role here. Use it to create paths and steps that are both practical and beautiful, providing a clear sense of direction for the feet while being pleasing to the eye. By helping to define entry areas, stone walls enhance the sense of shelter that makes these important spaces feel intimate and inviting rather than exposed and off-putting.

▲ COMPOSED OF GRANITE, this compass rose ensures that visitors to this coastal Maine home will never lose their bearings. The subtle variations in hue give the design a rich texture that complements the surrounding flagstone paving and cobbled columns.

▼ A PAIR OF GRANITE POSTS anchor this home's picket fence and mark the wide, straightforward pathway leading to the front door. The path's stone borders—set flush with the ground—echo the posts and help hold the bricks securely in place.

WHILE A WIDE, STRAIGHT PATH made of brick provides the main route from house to street, a longer, winding path of large stones recycled from an aging patio connects the front entry of this Toronto-area home to the driveway (left). The path provides a vibrant visual contrast with the formal brick architecture, while dividing the front yard into naturalistic planting areas. Visible from the street, the mortared fieldstone wall helps define the front entry (above).

Enchanting Front Entries

HERE ARE A FEW DESIGN TIPS to help dress up your front entry:

- Create a sense of enclosure. Whether created with shading branches and shrubs or with fences and walls, a front entry that enjoys a degree of privacy will feel sheltered and welcoming.

- Create a sense of passage. An entry is a transition from public to private space; gates, arbors, or even simple stone posts remind visitors that they're entering new territory.

- Create personality with plantings. Choose interesting trees, shrubs, and perennials that will thrive in your region and offer visitors year-round color and shape.

▲ AN INFORMAL STONE PATH passes through a small herb garden and entry gate before opening onto the breezeway of this Hudson River Valley home in upstate New York. Besides clearly indicating the location of the steps to visitors, the native fieldstone wall establishes the garden's boundaries.

◄ THIS SMALL TERRACE IS CONNECTED to neighboring garden spaces by the mixed use of brick and stone. Steps and changes in paving materials help signal transitions, while the landing just outside the kitchen door offers a place to pause and take in the view.

▲ A FORMAL WALKWAY paved with thermal-finish bluestone pavers cut into a diamond pattern frames the small kitchen garden of this historic New England farmhouse. Besides mirroring the layout of the garden, the simple trick of laying the field pavers on the diagonal visually widens the pathway.

...s and Transitions

...RTANCE OF THE AUTOMOBILE to most of our ..., it's surprising how unaccommodating ...scape designs are to its presence. Drive-... ...y cases, an afterthought, often too narrow to tur... ...t or too small to park extra cars. Their surfaces are usually ...nosen for the sake of economy and convenience rather than for how they relate to the style of the home or landscape. Transitions from driveway to house or yard are often muddled, with neither an obvious path to follow nor an obvious final destination. Stone and stonelike manufactured pavers are ideal for dressing up driveways and easing the transitions from car to home. Even when used on a relatively small scale—for example, widening a narrow driveway by adding a stone walkway along the edge—stone offers many practical and elegant solutions that will make your home more beautiful and inviting.

▲ BESIDES BEING EXTREMELY DURABLE, this granite cobblestone parking court has a neutral texture that draws attention to the sculpture it surrounds. The darker, contrasting stone dust used in the joints to help set the cobblestones emphasizes their color and their running bond pattern.

▲ IT ISN'T NECESSARY TO PAVE an entire driveway with cobble-stones; this abbreviated welcome mat helps define the entrance to this Maine home and the change from public to private space.

▲ THIS PEA STONE GRAVEL DRIVEWAY is framed by a border of Tennessee fieldstone. Small enough to compact firmly under tire treads or footsteps, the $1/2$-in.-dia. pea stones are also large enough that they stay in place and aren't easily tracked into the house.

▲ STONE PILLARS BUILT WITH LOCAL MATERIAL mark the transition from the driveway and clearly signal the entrance to this Baltimore residence. The pillars are capped with Pennsylvania bluestone to match the paving on the path and the series of short steps leading to the house.

▲ THE DRIVEWAY'S PRIMARY PAVING SURFACE is concrete but the spare, geometric grid of pavers adds a subtle accent to this California home's front yard landscape and logically directs visitors toward the front entry.

About Cobblestones

A TRADITIONAL PAVING MATERIAL—though not technically a paver due to thickness—cobblestones were once extensively used to cover city streets. Because they are so durable, many have been salvaged for reuse; an online search will reveal a number of sources for both European and American cobblestones, some that date back 400 years. Polished and worn from centuries of use, these granite cobblestones have an antique patina that may be perfect for your project.

Of course, quarries today produce new cobblestones, primarily out of granite but also from more expensive (but less durable) limestone. Colors vary depending on where the stone has been quarried, but white, gray, and rose granites are the most common. Sizes vary too, particularly if you're considering antique cobblestones, but the two most common are called regulation (4 in. by 5 in. by 9 in.) and jumbo (4 in. by 7 in. by 11 in.). Rock pitching is a process that gives cobblestones tumbled edges and makes them

look older. Prices vary widely, but start at about $3.50 per sq. ft. for the most common gray granite Belgian block cobblestones; expect to pay more than twice as much for limestone cobbles, while prices for salvaged cobblestones depend on their age and source.

▲ MADE FROM GRANITE, Belgian block cobblestones last for centuries and are available in colors ranging from rose to gray (left). Less common and considerably more expensive, limestone cobbles vary in durability depending on where they've been quarried; some may hold up well in a driveway, while others are best for paths only (right).

Borders

ON A PRACTICAL LEVEL, BORDERS THAT SEPARATE walking surfaces from planting areas prevent loose gravel from migrating into lawns and gardens and block soil and mulch so that pathways stay clean and neat. But borders can be a decorative element in their own right, enhancing a landscape's overall design. Unlike timbers or metal edgings, stone, brick, and cast concrete won't rot or rust, and while plastic edgings are more economical and easier to install, they don't have the substantial, natural look of stone or its close cousins. As you weigh your options, keep your landscape's character in mind. Neat and tidy formal landscape designs generally call for interlocking or mortared borders that hold grasses and ground covers in bounds. Informal designs invite encroachment; simple fieldstones or cobbles laid on edge have plenty of nooks and crannies that allow turf or ground covers to blur the boundaries between hard and soft surfaces.

▲ THIS MORTARED BORDER CLEARLY DEFINES the planting bed's boundary while being wide enough to double as a narrow secondary walking surface. The geometric collage of salvaged brick and variously shaped and colored flat stones provides an eye-catching texture.

▶ LIKE BURIED TREASURE, small stones unearthed while digging in the garden can be put to good use. Here they form a not-too-formal edging that defines the borders of a curving path while helping to unify the various parts of this woodland garden.

▲ TIGHTLY FITTED SQUARE AND RECTANGULAR stone pavers make a neatly geometric statement as they border this pea stone gravel parking area. Laid vertically, the toothy-textured edging stones create a clear boundary that helps hold back the mulch in the adjacent planting bed.

▲ THOUGH SIMPLE IN DESIGN, this border prevents garden mulch from spilling over into the driveway and gives the edges of both the driveway and the garden a finishing touch.

▲ BUILT WITH FLAT STONES and smaller river rocks left over from a more extensive landscaping project, this curbside walkway replaces lawn, provides a robust border for the planting bed, and offers firm and dry footing when entering or exiting a car parked in the street.

Credits

p. ii: Photo © Brian Vanden Brink, photographer 2005.

p. v: Photo © Lisa Romerein.

p. vi: (top) Photo © 2005 Carolyn L. Bates-carolynbates.com; (bottom) Photo © Eric Roth.

p. 1: (top left) Photo © Brian Vanden Brink, photographer 2005; (top right) Photo by Lee Anne White, © The Taunton Press, Inc.; (bottom left) Photo © davidduncanlivingston.com; (bottom right) Photo by Virginia Small, © The Taunton Press, Inc.; Garden design by Ed Snodgrass/Emory Knoll Farms, Street, Maryland.

p. 2: Photo © Eric Roth.

p. 3: (top) Photo © Lee Anne White; (bottom) Photo © Linda Svendsen.

Chapter 1

p. 4: Photo © Eric Roth; Design by Lou French, Vineyard Haven, MA.

p. 5: (left) Photo © Tim Street-Porter; (center & right) Photos © 2005 Carolyn L. Bates-carolynbates.com.

p. 6: (bottom) Photo by Steve Silk, © The Taunton Press, Inc.; Path/Garden Design by Valerie Easton, Lake Forest, WA; (top) Photo © Brian Vanden Brink, photographer 2005; Design by Horiuchi & Solien Inc., Falmouth, MA

p. 7: (left) Photo © Lee Anne White Design by Jeffrey Bale, Portland, OR; (right) Photo © Lee Anne White; Design by Stephen Carruthers, Portland, OR

p. 8: Photo © www.stevevierraphotography.com; Design by Kennedy & Co. Landscaping, Acton, MA.

p. 9: (top) Photos by Scott Phillips, © The Taunton Press, Inc.; (bottom) Photo by Jennifer Brown, © The Taunton Press, Inc.

p. 10: (left & top right) Photos © 2005 Carolyn L. Bates-carolynbates.com; Stonework by Paul Wieczoreck/Champlain Valley Landscaping, Hinesburg, VT; Garden of Marcia Pierce, Hinesburg, VT; Landscape Design by George and Joanna Zavis/Hannabelle Garden Center, Cambridge; (bottom right) Photo © Lee Anne White.

p. 11: Photo © Eric Roth.

p. 12: (top) Photos by Scott Phillips, © The Taunton Press, Inc.; (bottom) Photo © Eric Roth; Design by Lou French, Vineyard Haven, MA.

p. 13: Photo by Jennifer Benner, © The Taunton Press, Inc.; Design by Rob and Sue Denoncourt, Nantucket, MA.

p. 14: (top left) Photo © Lee Anne White; Design by Keith Geller, Seattle, WA; (bottom left) Photo © 2005 Carolyn L. Bates-carolynbates.com; Design by Clemens and Associates, Inc., Santa Fe, NM; (top right) Photo © Allan Mandell.

p. 15: Photo © 2005 Carolyn L. Bates-carolynbates.com; Garden of Marcia Pierce, Hinesburg, VT.

p. 16: (left) Photo by Vincent Laurence, © The Taunton Press, Inc.; (right) Photo by Allan Mandell, © The Taunton Press, Inc.; Design by Margaret de Haas van Dorsser, Portland, OR.

p. 17: (top) Photo by Jennifer Benner, © The Taunton Press, Inc.; (bottom) Photo by Lee Anne White, © The Taunton Press, Inc.

p. 18: (left) Photo by Steven Aitken, © The Taunton Press, Inc.; Design by Jim Scott, Montgomery, AL; (right top & bottom) Photos © Lee Anne White; Landscape design by Paula Refi, Atlanta, GA, Stonework by Rice & Clemons, Atlanta, GA; Garden of Barbara and Gordon Robinson, Atlanta, GA.

p.19: (top) Photo © Lisa Romerein; Design by Kyle Irwin/Botanik, Santa Barbara, CA; (bottom) Photo © Lee Anne White; Design by Juan Arzola/J.C. Enterprise Services, Weston, FL.

p. 20: (left) Photo by Virginia Small, © The Taunton Press, Inc.; Design by Tom Vetter, Portland, OR; (right top) Photo © Allan Mandell; Design by Jeffrey Bale, Portland, OR; (right bottom) Photo © 2005 Carolyn L. Bates-carolynbates.com; Design by Clemens and Associates, Inc., Santa Fe, NM.

p. 21: (top) Photo © Lee Anne White; Design by Dan Cleveland, Atlanta, GA; (bottom) Photo © Lee Anne White; Design by David Ellis/Ellis Landesign, Atlanta, GA.

p. 22: (top) Photo © Lee Anne White; Design/Construction by Michael Thilgen/Four Dimensions Landscape Company, Oakland, CA; (bottom) Photos © Brian Vanden Brink, photographer 2005; Design by Horiuchi & Solien Inc., Falmouth, MA.

p. 23: (top) Photo © 2005 Carolyn L. Bates-carolynbates.com; Design by Clemens and Associates, Inc., Santa Fe, NM; (bottom) Photo © Lisa Romerein; Design by Mary Lou Sorrell/Sorrell Design, Santa Barbara, CA.

p. 24: (top) Photo © Lisa Romerein; Design by Henry Lenny Design Studios, Carpenteria, CA; (bottom) Photo © davidduncanlivingston.com.

p. 25: (top) Photo © Lisa Romerein; Design by Paul Robbins Garden Design, Los Angeles, CA; (bottom) Photo © Lee Anne White; Design by Warren Simmonds/Simmonds & Associates, San Anselmo, CA; Construction by Four Dimensions Landscape Company, Oakland, CA.

p. 26: (top right) Photo © Lee Anne White; Design by C.D. Gann; (bottom left & right) Photos by Lee Anne White, © The Taunton Press; Design by Keith Geller, Seattle, WA.

p. 27: Photo by Steve Silk, © The Taunton Press, Inc.

p. 28: (left) Photo by Virginia Small, © The Taunton Press, Inc.; Design by Jeff Osser, Chesterfield, MO; (right) Photo © Brian Vanden Brink, photographer 2005; Design by Horiuchi & Solien Inc., Falmouth, MA.

p. 29: (top left & bottom left) Photos © Allan Mandell; (top right) Photo © Tim Street-Porter; Landscape Design by Pamela Burton and Company, Los Angeles, CA; Construction by Joe Conti/Macon Construction, Pacific Palisades, CA.

Chapter 2

p. 30: Photo © 2005 Carolyn L. Bates-carolynbates.com; Landscape Design by George and Joanna Zavis/Hannabelle Garden Center, Cambridge, VT.

p. 31: (left) Photo © www.stevevierra-photography.com; (center) Photo © Eric Roth; (right) Photo © Tim Street-Porter.

p. 32: (top) Photo by Lee Anne White, © The Taunton Press; (bottom) Photo © Eric Roth; Design by Lou French, Vineyard Haven, MA.

p. 33: Photo © Eric Roth.

p. 34: (left) Photo © Brian Vanden Brink, photographer 2005; Design by Horiuchi & Solien Inc., Falmouth, MA.; (right) Photo © Allan Mandell; Design by Jeffrey Bale, Portland, OR.

p. 35: (top) Photo © Lisa Romerein; Design by Paul Robbins Garden Design, Los Angeles, CA; (bottom) Photo © Lee Anne White; Design by Warren Simmonds/Simmonds & Associates, San Anselmo, CA.; Construction by Four Dimensions, Oakland, CA.

p. 36: (top left) Photo © Brian Vanden Brink, photographer 2005; Architectural Design by Whitten Architects, Portland, ME; Landscape Design by Catherine Court Landscape Gardens & Design, East Boothbay, ME; (top right) Photo © Tim Street-Porter; (bottom) Photo © Brian Vanden Brink, photographer 2005.

p. 37: Photo © Brian Vanden Brink, photographer 2005; Design by Horiuchi & Solien Inc., Falmouth, MA

p. 38: Photo © Lisa Romerein.

p. 39: (left) Photo © Tim Street-Porter; (right) Photo © Brian Vanden Brink, photographer 2005; Architectural Design by Polhemus Savery DaSilva Architects Builders, Chatham, MA; Landscape Design by Hawk Design Inc., Charlestown, MA; (bottom) Photos by Scott Phillips, © The Taunton Press, Inc.; Construction by Four Dimensions, Oakland, CA

p. 40: (left) Photo © davidduncanlivingston.com; (top right) Photo © Lisa Romerein; Design by Sloane and Greg Mann/Fibonnacci Design Group, Altadena, CA; (bottom right) Photo © Lisa Romerein; Design by Scott Shrader, Beverly Hills, CA.

p. 41: Photo © davidduncanlivingston.com.

p. 42: (left) Photo © Tim Street-Porter; (top right) Photo © Tim Street-Porter; (bottom right) Photo © Brian Vanden Brink, photographer 2005; Design by McMillen, Inc. New York, NY.

p. 43: (top) Photo © Lisa Romerein; Design by Paul Robbins Garden Design, Los Angeles, CA; (bottom) Photo © Halkin Photography; Design by Donald Billinkoff Architects, New York, NY.

p. 44: (top) Photo © davidduncanlivingston.com; (bottom) Photo © Brian Vanden Brink, photographer 2005.

p. 45: Photo © Allan Mandell; Design by Michael Schultz, Portland, OR.

p. 46: (top left) Photo © davidduncanlivingston.com; (top right) Photo © Lee Anne White; (bottom) Photo © Lee Anne White; Garden of Barbara Mitchell.

p. 47: (top left) Photo © 2005 Carolyn L. Bates-carolynbates.com; Design by Clemens and Associates, Inc., Santa Fe, NM; (top right) Photo © Tim Street-Porter; Design by Jarrett Hedborg, Los Angles, CA; (bottom) Photo © Tim Street-Porter; Landscape Design by Pamela Burton and Company, Los Angeles, CA; Construction by Joe Conti/Macon Construction, Pacific Palisades, CA.

p. 48: (top) Photo © Lee Anne White; Garden of Fred & Sallye Hooks, Atlanta, GA; (bottom right) Photo © Eric Roth; (bottom left) Photo © Brian Vanden Brink, photographer 2005.

p. 49: Photos by Lee Anne White, © The Taunton Press; Design by Kathryn MacDougald, Atlanta, GA.

p. 50: (top left) Photo © Lee Anne White; Design by Sandy Snyder, Denver, CO; (top right) Photo © 2005 Carolyn L. Bates-carolynbates.com; Garden by Colleen Steen, Fairfax, VT; (bottom) Photo by Jennifer Brown, © The Taunton Press; Design by Lucinda Hutson, Austin, TX.

p. 51: Photos by Steve Silk, © The Taunton Press, Inc.; Garden design by Verle Lessig, Chicago, IL; Construction by Four Dimensions, Oakland, CA.

p. 52: (top) Photo © Lisa Romerein; Design by Carla Melson, Los Angeles, CA; (bottom) Photo © Brian Vanden Brink, photographer 2005; Design by Horiuchi & Solien Inc., Falmouth, MA.

p. 53: Photo © Brian Vanden Brink, photographer 2005; Architectural Design by Van Dam Architecture & Design, Portland, ME; Stonework by George Couture, Bowdoinham, ME and Kevin O'Donnell, Nobleboro, ME.

p. 54: (top left & right) Photos © Brian Vanden Brink, photographer 2005; Design by Horiuchi & Solien Inc., Falmouth, MA; (bottom) Photo © 2005 Carolyn L. Bates-carolynbates.com; Design by Keith Wagner/Wagner McCann Studio, Burlington, VT.

p. 55: (top) Photo © Lisa Romerein; (bottom) Photo © www.stevevierraphotography.com; Design by Kennedy & Co. Landscaping, Acton, MA.

Chapter 3

p. 56: Photo by Virginia Small, © The Taunton Press, Inc.; Garden design by Ed Snodgrass/Emory Knoll Farms, Street, MD.

p. 57: (left) Photo © Lee Anne White; Design by Malcolm George; (center) Photo © 2005 Carolyn L. Bates-carolynbates.com; Design by Andrea Morgante, Hinesburg, VT; Stonework by David Mason, Starksboro, VT; (right) Photo © Linda Svendsen.

p. 58: Photos by Photo © Brian Vanden Brink, photographer 2005; Architectural Design by Scholz & Barclay Architects, Camden, ME; Stonework by Dan Eaton/Landscapes, Inc., Camden, ME.

p. 59: (top) Photo © Tim Street-Porter; (bottom) Photo © Linda Svendsen.

p. 60: (left) Photo © Brian Vanden Brink, photographer 2005; Design by Horiuchi & Solien Inc., Falmouth, MA; (right top) Photo © Brian Vanden Brink, photographer 2005; Landscape Design by Oehme, van Sweden & Associates, Washington, D.C.; Design by IOI Inc., Boston, MA; (right center) Photo © Eric Roth; design by Lou French, Vineyard Haven, MA; (right bottom) Photo © 2005 Carolyn L. Bates-carolynbates.com; Landscape design by Kircen Seibert/Broadleaf Landscape, Waitsfield, VT; Stonework by Paul Wieczorek/Champlain Valley Landscaping, Hinesburg, VT.

p. 61: Photo © Mark Samu/Courtesy Hearst Magazines.

p. 62: (left) Photo by Jennifer Brown, © The Taunton Press, Inc.; Design by Steve Biskey and Mark Watters, Parksville, NY; (top right) Photo © 2005 Carolyn L. Bates-carolynbates.com; Design by Paul Wieczoreck/Champlain Valley Landscaping, Hinesburg, VT; Garden of Marcia Pierce, Hinesburg, VT; (bottom right) Photo courtesy Michelle Derviss; Landscape design by Michelle Derviss; Stonework by Miguel Chavez, Novato, CA.

p. 63: (left) Photo © davidduncanlivingston.com; (right top) Virginia Small; Garden design by Ed Snodgrass/Emory Knoll Farms, Street, Maryland; (right bottom) Lee Anne White, Photo © The Taunton Press; Design by Jeni Webber, Oakland, CA.

p. 64: (top) Photo © Brian Vanden Brink, photographer 2005; Architectural Design by Whitten Architects, Portland, ME; Landscape Design by Catherine Court Landscape Gardens & Design, East Boothbay, ME; (bottom) Photo © 2005 Carolyn L. Bates-carolynbates.com; Landscape Design by Ruskey Knauf Associates, Stowe, VT; Stonework by Mark Moody, Elmore, VT.

p. 65: Photos © 2005 Carolyn L. Bates-carolynbates.com; Design by Andrea Morgante, Hinesburg, VT; Stonework by David Mason, Starksboro, VT.

p. 66: (top) Photo © Brian Vanden Brink, photographer 2005; Design by Horiuchi & Solien Inc., Falmouth, MA;

(bottom) Photo © Lee Anne White; Design by David Ellis/Ellis Landesign, Atlanta, GA.

p. 67: (top) Photo © Lee Anne White; Design by David Thorne Landscape Architect, Oakland, CA; (bottom) Photo © Linda Svendsen.

p. 68: (top) Photo © Brian Vanden Brink, photographer 2005; Design by Jefferson B. Riley and Charles G. Mueller/Centerbrook Architects and Planners, Centerbrook, CT; Stonework by Ken Makely; (bottom) Photo by Steven Aitken, © The Taunton Press, Inc.; Design by Jim Scott, Montgomery, AL.

p. 69: (top) Photo © Brian Vanden Brink, photographer 2005; Architectural Design by Van Dam Architecture & Design, Portland, ME; Stonework by George Couture, Bowdoinham, ME and Kevin O'Donnell, Nobleboro, ME; (bottom) Photo © Lee Anne White; Design by Michelle Derviss.

p. 70: (left) Photo © Brian Vanden Brink, photographer 2005; Design by Robinson + Grisaru Architecture, Brooklyn, NY; (right) Photo © Brian Vanden Brink, photographer 2005; Design by Horiuchi & Solien Inc., Falmouth, MA.

p. 71: Photo © Brian Vanden Brink, photographer 2005; Design by John Morris Architects, Camden, ME .

p. 72: (left photos) Photo © 2005 Carolyn L. Bates-carolynbates.com; Design by Clemens and Associates, Inc., Santa Fe, NM; (top right) Photo © Lee Anne White; Design by Jeffrey Bale, Portland, OR; (bottom right) Photo © Lee Anne White; Design by Michael Thilgen/Four Dimensions Landscape Company, Oakland, CA.

p. 73: Photo © Brian Vanden Brink, photographer 2005; Design by Jefferson B. Riley and Charles G. Mueller/Centerbrook Architects and Planners, Centerbrook, CT; Stonework by Ken Makely.

p. 74: (top left & right) Photos © Linda Svendsen; (bottom) Photo © 2005 Carolyn L. Bates-carolynbates.com; Design by Clemens and Associates, Inc., Santa Fe, NM.

p. 75: Photo © Brian Vanden Brink, photographer 2005; Design by Horiuchi & Solien Inc., Falmouth, MA.

p. 76: (left) Courtesy Zaretsky and Associates, Inc.; (right) Photo © Linda Svendsen.

p. 77: Photo © Lee Anne White; Design by Paula Refi, Atlanta, GA.

Chapter 4

p. 78: Photo © davidduncanlivingston.com; Design by Jerry Gunnelson, WI.

p. 79: (left) Photo © Lee Anne White; (center) Photo by Todd Meier, © The Taunton Press, Inc.; (right) Photo © Brian Vanden Brink, photographer 2005, photographer Photo © 2005.

p. 80: (top) Photo © davidduncanlivingston.com ; (bottom) Photo by Virginia Small, © The Taunton Press, Inc.; Design by Jeff Osser, Chesterfield, MO.

p. 81: (top) Photo © 2005 Carolyn L. Bates-carolynbates.com; Design by Andrea Morgante, Hinesburg, VT; Stonework by David Mason, Starksboro, VT; (bottom) Photo by Lee Anne White, ©The Taunton Press; Garden of Karin Overbeck, Wisconsin.

p. 82: (top) Photo © Lee Anne White; Design by Mark Fockele/Fockele Garden Company, Gainesville, GA; (bottom) Photo © Lee Anne White; Garden of Bernadine & Jean-Paul Richard, Atlanta, GA.

p. 83: (top) Photo © davidduncanlivingston.com; (bottom) Photo © Brian Vanden Brink, photographer 2005.

p. 84: (top and bottom) Photos © 2005 Carolyn L. Bates-carolynbates.com; Design by Ken Mills/Insight Design, Consulting, and Architectural Landscaping, Winooski, VT.

p. 85: (left) Photo © Allan Mandell; (right) Photo © Mark Samu; Design by Dave Barrows/Access Builders, Latham, NY.

p. 86: (left) Photo © Lee Anne White; Design by Keith Geller, Seattle, WA; (top right) Photo by Todd Meier, © The Taunton Press, Inc.; Design by Gordon Hayward, Putney, VT; (bottom right) Photo © Eric Roth; Design by Lou French, Vineyard Haven, MA.

p. 87: (left) Photo © Lee Anne White; Design by David Ellis/Ellis Landesign, Atlanta, GA; (right) Photo © 2005 Carolyn L. Bates-carolynbates.com; Labyrinth Design by Lynn Hartwood, Ontario, Canada; Landscape Design by Ken Mills/Insight Design, Consulting, and Architectural Landscaping, Winooski, VT.

p. 88: (top left) Photo © 2005 Carolyn L. Bates-carolynbates.com; Design by David and Matthew Furney, Lincoln, VT; (top right) Photo © davidduncanlivingston.com; (bottom) Photo by Virginia Small, © The Taunton Press, Inc.; Design by Jeff Osser, Chesterfield, MO.

For More Great Design Ideas, Look for These and Other Taunton Press Books Wherever Books are Sold.

NEW KITCHEN IDEA BOOK
1-56158-693-5
Product #070773
$19.95 U.S.
$27.95 Canada

NEW BATHROOM IDEA BOOK
1-56158-692-7
Product #070774
$19.95 U.S.
$27.95 Canada

NEW KIDSPACE IDEA BOOK
1-56158-694-3
Product #070776
$19.95 U.S.
$27.95 Canada

NEW BUILT-INS IDEA BOOK
1-56158-673-0
Product #070755
$19.95 U.S.
$27.95 Canada

TRIM IDEA BOOK
1-56158-710-9
Product #070786
$19.95 U.S.
$27.95 Canada

TILE IDEA BOOK
1-56158-709-5
Product #070785
$19.95 U.S.
$27.95 Canada

TAUNTON'S HOME STORAGE IDEA BOOK
1-56158-676-5
Product #070758
$19.95 U.S.
$27.95 Canada

TAUNTON'S FAMILY HOME IDEA BOOK
1-56158-729-X
Product #070789
$19.95 U.S.
$27.95 Canada

TAUNTON'S HOME WORKSPACE IDEA BOOK
ISBN 1-56158-701-X
Product #070783
$19.95 U.S.
$27.95 Canada

BACKYARD IDEA BOOK
1-56158-667-6
Product #070749
$19.95 U.S.
$27.95 Canada

POOL IDEA BOOK
1-56158-764-8
Product #070825
$19.95 U.S.
$27.95 Canada

DECK & PATIO IDEA BOOK
1-56158-639-0
Product #070718
$19.95 U.S.
$27.95 Canada

TAUNTON'S FRONT YARD IDEA BOOK
1-56158-519-X
Product #070621
$19.95 U.S.
$27.95 Canada

FOR MORE INFORMATION VISIT OUR WEBSITE AT www.taunton.com